Yankee Si!

Photo by Dementi Studio

DR. J. CALVITT CLARKE, Founder and International
Director of Christian Children's Fund, Inc.

YANKEE SI!

The Story of Dr. J. Calvitt Clarke
and his 36,000 Children

By *EDMUND W. JANSS*

With a Foreword by

Dr. Daniel A. Poling

New York, 1961

WILLIAM MORROW & COMPANY

To those who have helped to make America loved

Library of Congress Catalog Card Number 61-16608

Contents

Foreword by
Daniel A. Poling

BEFORE the "Red Terror" came down on China, the journal of which I am Editor, *Christian Herald*, had two long-established orphanages in Fukien Province at Foochow; also one of the largest industrial schools in Asia which was opened more than thirty years ago. It was when the growing tensions made it apparent that we could no longer continue the effective supervision of our work in Foochow that we made a careful investigation of the Richmond institution then known as China's Children Fund. What that investigation revealed caused us to turn over to this fund the administration of our entire program in China. We have never regretted the decision. When our million-dollar properties were confiscated, when our work was ended on the mainland and when our children were scattered, because the Christian Children's Fund made it possible, we moved to Formosa where we now have two orphanages. One of these is the first foundling home opened on that remarkable island. Our home in Hong Kong, Faith-Love Orphanage, with its nearly 200 girls and boys, is the largest of these three. More recently we have opened, with the Christian Children's Fund, an orphanage in Korea.

The Christian Children's Fund, with Dr. J. Calvitt Clarke as Founder and International Director, with its 418 homes for orphans scattered around the world in forty-eight countries, has become the most unique and responsible agency in the whole field. Formerly the China's Children Fund, it had forty-five homes in China proper when the Communists took over. They confiscated everything. The boys from fourteen years up were taken into the army. The majority of the orphanages were closed. Others were continued as "Children's Productive Institutes." Men and women who had given their lives to this work saw a tragic spectacle on "Liberation Day," October 1, 1950, when the children they had loved and cherished were sent marching under banners of hatred and with anti-God slogans through the streets of Chinese cities from Canton to Peiping. But now the Christian Children's Fund, in addition to 93 orphanages and homes in Korea, has 60 similar institutions in Japan. There is also a thoroughly modern Home on the Island of Okinawa, for which American chaplains raised and contributed the initial $10,000. This is now totally staffed and supported by Christian Children's Fund. The seventeen orphanages and projects owned by or affiliated with CCF in Hong Kong care for 4,700 orphans of the total 7,000 who are the wards of both Catholic and Protestant institutions. In this most famous of England's Crown Colonies, the official reports of the Government devote appreciative pages to Christian Children's Fund and its program.

In India, I have visited several times at Alwaye Settlement in Kerala Province. Here is one of the most effective answers to Communism I observed in all Asia. Here is not only a Home with the usual school facilities. There are also an experimental farm, a dairy, weaving shops, carpentry and other workshops.

In 1953, as a member of the Board of Christian Children's Fund, I had the privilege of declaring open a new primary school which is filling a longstanding need in the area. At the same function the foundation stone for a modern technical high school was laid by the Chief Minister of the State.

The children's schooling includes Bible teaching, which is emphasized in Christian Children's Fund Homes throughout the world. Nearly all of the boys and girls at Alwaye Settlement are from the depressed classes—the lowest castes. A year at this Home destroys their inferiority complex. Intelligent and in spite of their background possessed of initiative, they train into capable young citizens of India. To eyes unaccustomed to the marks of caste, the boys and girls I have seen there, though more darkly shaded, were just as yours and mine.

What more can I say? I have visited, too, in many of the ninety-plus CCF Homes in Korea. Several years ago I saw the "little boy who couldn't smile." You will probably never forget that indescribably pathetic little five-year-old whose picture first appeared in *Life Magazine* on August 18, 1951. Lee Kong Yang, aged five, had lost everything—mother, father, sisters, brothers—in the war. His eyes reflected the terrors of a war that should never have been, and he was half-starved. A few months after the first picture, a second appeared. In that later portrait a GI, stationed near Taegu, was holding a newly-happy lad with a broad grin on his filled-out face. And that broad grin has continued to widen over the ensuing years for Lee became one of the hundreds of children who have been cared for in the Taegu Bo Yook Won Home, which is affiliated with Christian Children's Fund. He is typical of the more than 12,000 Korean children who, like "the little boy who couldn't smile," owe their smiles to Christian Children's Fund and its thousands of sponsors.

Actually, 20 per cent of all children in institutions in South Korea are being helped in this way. Christian Children's Fund is by far the largest welfare project for children in South Korea. In fact, with a budget of nearly one million dollars annually in Korea, it is as large as most of the missionary organizations with which it cooperates. According to recent figures on orphans and orphanages in Korea released by the Ministry of Social Affairs of the Republic of Korea, there are at least 60,000 children in institutions. But, even today, there are at least 25,000 who remain outside Homes and who desperately need care. No single private agency, and indeed no government organization can fully cope with this number of children. Christian Children's Fund remains the brightest spot, however, because it was there first with the most and it is expanding as the needs continue.

In a recent round-the-world trip, I felt the fingers of thousands of little children tangle in mine. Japanese and Korean children, Taiwanese children, Chinese children in Hong Kong, children in India from the high Himalayas to the burning south, Arab babies in Jordan, Armenian babies in Lebanon, the little ones of Italy in Naples and the tragic orphans who have fled from the Red purge in East Germany. These youngsters by the thousands were in CCF orphanages.

In Berlin and West Germany, the Christian Children's Fund supports, through its "adoption" plan, over 1,300 of the orphaned or deserted boys and girls of this "Red Scourge." In Austria and Switzerland hundreds of young "escapees" from Hungary and other Communist regimes have flocked to CCF Homes.

"But what of the future?" people ask me. And surely it is to the future, this prophetic future, that CCF's orphan "adoption" and the support of the homes for the orphaned, this people-to-people vast enterprise, contributes. It was the Master Baby-Lover of the world, Himself, who said, "A little child shall lead them."

Shall we not hope and pray that these children of the bloody purges shall lead us toward that brotherhood and unity which centers at last in God's Fatherhood?

New York, 1961.

ONE

Yankee, Si!

For over half a century now, J. Calvitt Clarke has steadily become a more widely known and beloved international figure. A Presbyterian minister himself, he has not only the backing of his own denomination but the ardent support of people from every race and creed. Protestant, Catholic and Jew, Buddhist, Moslem and Hindu have shared their time, money and effort for his cause. The founder of the Christian Children's Fund, Dr. Clarke is in a very real sense "the un-ugly American."

His cause, as most people know, is the care, shelter and feeding of over 36,000 children in forty-eight countries and 418 orphanages and projects. His work has been the means of making good citizens out of delinquent boys and of lifting hopeless girls out of an uncertain future. Thousands of tiny babies left on doorsteps, in alleys and in railway stations to die have been succored in the nick of time.

Although the Christian Children's Fund is largely a Protestant organization, children of every background receive care in its homes. A direct descendant of Mohammed resides in a Lebanese CCF Home, while another child tracing his ancestry straight back to Confucius receives CCF care in a Hong Kong project. Buddhist children are tended in one of the

1

Korean Homes and Shintoists in a Japanese orphanage. Among the American Indians under CCF care are more than a few whose background is Roman Catholic. Negro children are aided in Virginia and South Carolina as well as in Africa. Leprous children are assisted in Thailand, blind youngsters in Formosa and deaf children in Hong Kong. Juvenile beggars and thieves from the streets of Seoul have been rescued and rehabilitated by the score, taught to read and write, and trained in manual vocations.

Dr. Clarke's description of Christian Children's Fund has been the motto of his life: "Administering to the physical, mental and spiritual needs of children of all races and creeds." In this many of his fellow Americans have gladly seconded him. Helping youngsters whose minds have been twisted by misfortune and hopelessness, homelessness and disease, he has encouraged them back to a life with a happy future. It has been his heartfelt purpose, in the CCF Homes, to give the best opportunity possible to all, and he has, of course, been abetted in this aim by many eager friends and co-workers.

Though he has given much, and through him many others have given much, he has accomplished it by the policy of never *asking* for funds. Dr. Clarke himself has put it: "I never ask for gifts. I only tell the real conditions and needs." His own feeling about giving is mirrored in the story he told me of the polite Hindu who, when he places a coin in a beggar's cup, always murmurs, "Thank you for giving me the privilege to give." On the same occasion he remarked, "I am an old and somewhat tired 'beggar.' For fifty years I have held out my hand in this fashion. It was always of others' needs that I talked, but I could hardly blame people if they thought of me as an annoying person. But our contributors have been very kind to me and my little family now numbers over 36,000 CCF-assisted children around the world. May their gifts bring them happiness!"

As I sat and listened to him, I suddenly realized that of course his hundreds of thousands of friends have identified themselves with him, and have, in the process, become "un-ugly Americans." And in the hearts of a host of folk throughout the world, there is love for America because of Dr. Clarke and his friends.

Typically, he has waved personal credit aside feeling that it belonged to his beloved America and its kindly citizens. Certainly his work and theirs is a power for great good. Someone rightly said, "The work of Christian Children's Fund has done more for America's prestige abroad than $10,000,-000,000 in armament assistance!"

Recognition for his work and the work of his friends has come somewhat late in his life, but now the voices of the great and near-great rise in ever-increasing volume.

In the spring of 1957, their Imperial Highnesses, the Emperor and Empress of Japan received Dr. and Mrs. Clarke with great honor at the Palace. For almost an hour the Emperor spoke of his gratitude for CCF's work in that country. "With over 10 per cent of Japan's orphanages under the care of Christian Children's Fund, we owe a great debt to you," said the Emperor. "We want to do all we can for our orphan children and are helping them as you know. But Japan is not rich and we deeply appreciate all that Christian Children's Fund is doing to help our little ones!"

As a fitting sequel to this high occasion, in early 1961, Dr. Clarke received a communication from the Japanese Consul-General which said:

It is a great pleasure for me to inform you that His Majesty the Emperor has conferred upon you the Fourth Class of the Order of the Sacred Treasure in recognition of your contributions to the advancement of child welfare in Japan.

This decoration for distinguished service was awarded to you at the recommendation of the Ministry of Health and Welfare, on the occasion of the Centennial of Japanese-American Relations.

Consul-General Mitsuo Tanaka went on to request that Dr. Clarke be decorated in person at the Japanese consulate in New York. And on Monday, March 13, 1961, the International Director of CCF was decorated with this high award. The "Patent of Decoration" reads:

> The Fourth Class of the Order of the Sacred Treasure, is hereby conferred upon Dr. J. Calvitt Clarke, American citizen, by His Majesty, the Emperor of Japan.
>
> In witness thereof, the Seal of State has been affixed to these presents at the Imperial Palace. This day, the Twenty-Third of the Twelfth Month of the Thirty-Fifth Year of Showa (1960).

Personally signed by Prime Minister Hayato Ikeda, it expressed the appreciation of a grateful people. When Dr. Clarke travelled in Japan, receptions and teas were given in his honor by mayors, government officials and civic leaders throughout the nation.

Similarly, visiting Korea in 1958, he was met at the airport by dignitaries from many provinces as well as from the national government. Banners of welcome were strung across the main streets of Seoul and over the principal bridge. Invited to the Presidential Mansion by President and Mrs. Syngman Rhee, he was awarded the Ribbon of Honor by that venerable patriot. In conveying the award, President Rhee read the following citation:

> In recognition and appreciation of outstanding and meritorious Christian service rendered to Korea, the President of the Republic of Korea, by authority vested in him by the Constitution of the Republic hereby commends Dr. J. Calvitt Clarke.
>
> The Christian Children's Fund, founded and wisely directed by Dr. Clarke, came to Korea in 1948 to provide urgently

needed care for children orphaned by war and suffering from the aftermath of war. With selfless devotion, Dr. Clarke gave careful attention to the welfare of our children and as a result of his nobel and arduous efforts 10,000 or more children in seventy-six institutions throughout Korea have benefited from the good work of the Christian Children's Fund.

Dr. Clarke's outstanding service in behalf of children whose lives were menaced by war is in the finest traditions and practices of democratic countries, and will always be remembered with admiration and deepest appreciation by the people of Korea.

In characteristic fashion, Dr. Clarke replied to the President, "All the credit for this goes to our many American sponsors!"

After the ceremony, a police escort led him through Seoul's city streets with sirens sounding, while crowds with flags lined the sidewalks. Dr. Clarke commented later, "I felt like a small boy going to a fire!"

On his return to this country, Dr. Clarke shared his experiences and honors with his sponsors, whom he felt deserved those honors too. "Appreciation for what America is doing?" Dr. Clarke answered his own question. "It could hardly have been louder, more prolonged or more enthusiastic. And in private conversations it was almost solemn, it was so genuine and sincere."

Madame Chiang Kai-shek received Dr. and Mrs. Clarke for tea at the Presidential Residence in Taiwan (Formosa). Madame Chiang expressed her own and the General's deep appreciation for the interest that CCF had always maintained in China, beginning with the years on the China mainland and then later moving with the government and the refugees to Taiwan, increasing work already established there.

The President of the Philippines extended warmest congratulations on the opening of yet another CCF Home— The Children's Garden in Manila. Since its erection this

Home has gained such a fine reputation that it has become a model used by the Government in establishing new orphanages throughout the Islands.

In Hong Kong, a luncheon for thirty outstanding guests was given in honor of Dr. and Mrs. Clarke by the Governor and Lady Grantham. Again, the same note was sounded, "We are so appreciative of our American friends!"

Asked for his reaction on CCF's reputation in Europe and the Near East, Dr. Clarke said, "It was the same wherever we went—lasting thanks to America. But best of all, really, was the way the little children themselves thanked us and wanted us to say thank-you to their sponsors in America!"

Just what, someone might ask, were they so thankful for?

Perhaps the best answer to this question can be found in the true story of little Amala. This is how she told it, a short time ago, in her halting fashion.

"I think I am six or seven. I'm not sure. I know I was born in Pakistan. My father was a good farmer. He owned his farm of two acres. Even though he was a Christian, everybody liked him. He could even read and write some. It was something about religion that made him sell his farm. Then we started for a place called Calcutta. Refugees were even on the roofs of the train. So father decided we would walk.

"One morning when I woke up where we were sleeping beside the road, my mother was trying to do something to my father's arm. She said, 'A thief broke it last night and stole all our money!' Then it got hard to walk and father's arm got all big and green looking. After a few days—I guess it was—he fell and mother pushed his body over the side of the road and put some rocks on him. We both cried a lot and started walking again. But we had nothing to eat and we stumbled a lot. I was so hungry. I even ate grass and mother pulled some bark off trees. We both ate that. I even tried to catch bugs to eat, although I had always been afraid of them before.

"We even crawled some. But we finally got to Calcutta. There were hundreds of refugees in the railroad station. Each family had a space on the floor big enough for a blanket. We had one left—mother had covered father with the other before she put the stones on him. They gave us some food. I ate it fast, but it made me sick. Once a day we got it—a sort of soup with things in it. Mother cried because she was proud, but she let me go out to beg. There were so many others. Some days I didn't get anything at all. But I found a place way off where I did better, even got some annas. I came back to mother to show her what I had.

"One night when I came back she was gone. The woman whose place was next to ours told me my mother would be back. But her husband said, 'You should tell the child. She died and they took her away.' I went back to begging next morning. I stayed on the streets now but I was always hungry and I cried a lot. I got sick and thought I would die and I was glad. But a woman picked me up and got her dress dirty carrying me. But she only smiled and put me in an automobile. I'd never been in one before and now I'm here in this Home with other children. Sometimes I laugh to myself and say I really did die and came here to heaven—and to this lady who is a friend of Jesus."

Amala and her friends are deeply grateful, and there are many of them. The ultimate source of their help may well be a biblical verse that Calvitt Clarke heard when he himself was a little boy. He heard it first from the lips of a great pastor in Brooklyn, a man by the name of S. Parkes Cadman. The words of the verse were: "Let the little ones come unto Me and forbid them not." He still remembers those words every day and so do thousands of other Americans. The world says "thanks" and each American is no longer so ugly.

TWO

A Boy Grows In Brooklyn

NURTURED in the principle of family love, the Clarkes of Brooklyn's Clinton Avenue went forth to share this principle with others. Years later, the youngest child, Calvitt, even more than the others, was to spread the "family theme" across a world. Every homeless waif whom his life could touch would be "adopted" and warmed at his global hearthside.

The youngest of four, Calvitt was not robust as a small child. Perhaps this is what early made him into a dreamer. But these dreams were to prove more powerful than bullets. Born on June 30, 1887, he entered a rapidly changing world. Just eight months prior to that time, a great statue had been unveiled within a few miles of his birthplace. On its pedestal appeared the words, "Give me your tired, your poor, your huddled masses. . ." It may have been prophetic that the statue's torch began to glow for needy people about the time young Calvitt appeared. A new hope was beginning to gleam in that year also, because America was just climbing out of one of her great depressions.

It was a fine day indeed when two refugees from Ireland's "huddled masses" came to live in the brownstone house on one of Brooklyn's stylish cobbled streets. Their names were Annie and Ellen and though they were hired as servant girls they were quickly "adopted" into the Clarke family. Calvitt, as the "baby," sat nightly on Annie's capacious lap in the basement kitchen. The tales of leprechauns and Irish kings made a vivid impression. Perhaps some of his ability as a gifted storyteller was born in that kitchen on Clinton Avenue.

Some of Calvitt's happiest recollections were of excursions to Coney Island, Manhattan Beach or Glen Island in the company of his mother, two brothers, and sister Mary, with Annie and Ellen carrying a sandwich hamper.

On one such outing Calvitt remembers that his mother eyed an unexpected sandwich hamper with a start. "I—I'm afraid you've gone to too much trouble, Annie," she said kindly. For, after all, they had come here partly to enjoy the shore dinners for which Glen Island was famous.

"But, ma'am," gentle Annie countered, "little Calvitt—you only know what he eats in the dining room. You should see him in my kitchen!" She smiled knowingly and, sure enough, her concern was vindicated. The hamper was empty when the boat returned to the pier and one small boy could take the credit.

At the beach, Calvitt loved to wander along the seafoam, searching for shells or watching the rolling surf. Sometimes he and middle brother Robert would stand hand-in-hand gazing at the great liners and schooners as they entered New York's lower bay. Together they would dream of the day when they might sail to distant lands. Happily hidden from both of their young eyes was Robert's untimely end. Twenty-five years later he would go down with the steamer *Eastland* in the terrible tragedy on the Chicago River. With him would go his beloved wife and child along with 809 others in the churning mud.

No doubt some of Calvitt's love for travel and the sea began here at the shore. In his late teens (during a summer interval from college), he even qualified as an able-bodied seaman on a freighter in Lake Superior (a vocation that he did not pursue farther, fortunately for thousands of thousands of children). Part of his appetite for faraway places may also have derived from his mother whose forebears were New London sea-captains.

Calvitt's father (whose name was also J. Calvitt) died when his youngest was still a small boy. He had been a successful broker on the Exchange and was a member of a distinguished southern family in which the legal profession had been traditional for generations. His great-grandfather, Joshua Giles Clarke, was First Chancellor of Mississippi. The family still possesses an old French Bible used by his grandfather, Judge J. Calvitt Clarke I, in swearing in witnesses appearing in his court in the French Quarter of New Orleans.

As a lad, Calvitt evidenced other inclinations. He was rather frail until his middle teens. "I was so thin in those days," he chuckles, "that if the Lord hadn't given me an Adam's apple I'd have had no shape at all." Due to his poor health, he was inclined to be meditative and introspective.

Largely because of this, he did not enter sports until his college years—one reason he has never played a game of baseball. "I somehow never developed much interest in it," he says quizzically. "In fact, to this day, I have never seen a big-league game!" As his health improved during early adolescence, however, he developed an avid interest in two other typically American games. They were football and basketball. Even now he keeps track of the scores in these sports and watches games on television when he can.

In his boyhood, young Calvitt wandered the quiet Brooklyn streets of his neighborhood. As he walked and wandered in the shade of the maples and elms, he did a lot of serious thinking—though also his mind conjured up "rather fantastic things," he recalls. After his father's death, the family lived with his grandmother, and despite their loss it was a warm family atmosphere, one in which he could build many dreams and ideals in complete security. It was at this time that his strongest childhood influence became prominent—his religious life.

When he was about ten, Calvitt began attending the large meetings sponsored by Brooklyn's Central YMCA, held every Sunday in the old Orpheum Theatre. These made a profound impression on his searching mind. *"The Brooklyn Daily Eagle,"* he later recalled, "carried a whole page of sermons every Monday morning that had been preached the day before by New York's pulpit giants." Charles Henry Parkhurst, the crusading New York minister was at his zenith then, and T. DeWitt Talmage, the preacher with the graphic tongue, was still on the scene. "Perhaps my favorite, though," he says, "was Newell Dwight Hillis—although, of course, I greatly admired my own pastor, S. Parkes Cadman. Dr. Cadman baptized me as a baby and later guided me in several important decisions."

"In the 1930's," he later recalled, "because a friend of mine was to be the speaker, I went back to the Central YMCA and attended a Sunday afternoon meeting. It was a great shock and disappointment to me to find that the crowds of thousands, which I recalled from my youth, had dwindled to twenty or thirty sad and tired-looking people. Brooklyn was no longer the 'city of churches'!"

In his fourteenth year, a restlessness gripped Calvitt. The world of blackboards, chalk and erasers suddenly became unreal to him. Despite his mother's protests, he says, "I dropped out of school. For some reason, I disliked it heartily!"

Casting about for something "practical," he ventured into the publishing field. He went to work in Manhattan, in the American branch of a London publisher by the name of John Lane, The Bodley Head, whose offices were then at 70 Fifth Avenue in an old building that has long since been torn down.

In those halcyon days, the horse-drawn Fifth Avenue Coaches traversed that thoroughfare as far as 110th Street. On their return trip they clip-clopped under Washington Arch and made a U-turn in the Square, a maneuver that their gas-driven descendants still perform.

Calvitt's salary on that job commenced at the rate of three dollars a week. From that princely sum, he had to deduct one dollar and twenty cents weekly for carfare. Morning and night he rode the clanging cars of the Fulton Street "L" to the Manhattan side of the Brooklyn Bridge for a nickel. Then descending the stairs of the East Side Subway, for another nickel he rode north to Fourteenth Street where he disembarked and trudged westward and southward to 70 Fifth Avenue. After such expenses, there was never much left in Calvitt's pockets.

Footing the lunch bill was sometimes a problem. In those "easy days," however, there was a restaurant significantly named "The Challenge." For fifteen cents one could purchase a meal of soup, meat, two vegetables, dessert and coffee or milk. Sometimes he splurged and ate there. More often, however, especially at the end of the week, he was to be found at the corner push-wagon where the noonday meal consisted of roll, frankfurter, sauerkraut and mustard. "On my word of honor," he declares, "this cost me two cents!" Calvitt had very independent ideas and wanted to "pay his own way."

Thoughtful and introspective, he began early to carry the weight of the world on his shoulders. His youthful foray into business made him aware of things he had never known in his sheltered life. He became conscious of the hardships that many of his fellow workers were experiencing in those days when one of the great depressions was sweeping the land. He sometimes wandered down to Mulberry and other streets in the tenement district and there experienced his first concern at the way others lived. The harsh lives of his contemporaries, the tenement children, was a shock to the sensitive boy reared in an atmosphere of love and security. . . . Forces were at work to make him the Pied Piper he later became.

Calvitt did not remain long in the publishing business. Two of his cousins owned summer cottages at Point O'Woods on Fire Island. Close by them was the summer home of Charles W. Hand, at that time treasurer of the Presbyterian Board of Foreign Missions. On one of his many visits to his relatives, he met Dr. Hand and soon found himself "hired-away-from" the Lane Publishing Company. For three years, his place of employment became 156 Fifth Avenue, several blocks north of his former office. "It is true," he said, "I made a little more money working for the Presbyterian Mission Board. But I still had to make frequent lunchtime visits to the frankfurter stand, nor was I ever able to plunge in Wall Street investments!"

His days as a "business man" soon drew to a close, however. The persuasion of a worried mother combined with his own innate good sense to make him decide that he should complete his schooling. At that time, the shadow of the great Dwight L. Moody still lay across the land, although that fiery personage had gone to his reward in 1899. One of the reminders of his organizing ability was the Mount Hermon School for Boys at Northfield, Massachusetts. Mrs. Clarke urged Calvitt to try a year or so there. Eager to get back to books and academic life, Calvitt willingly packed his bag and headed north. One can picture him descending from the steam cars of the old Boston and Maine at Mount Hermon Station, and ascending the hill to the school. It was late September, with frost beginning to touch the maples with red, and quiet voices seemed to speak to the lad's imagination of big things that were "like dreams in one's sleep—impossible but happening."

It was at Mount Hermon that many of Calvitt's basic convictions were finally set. His theology was to go through several adjustments in later life, but the essential thought-forms would remain. As he finished his preparatory education there, a determination to train for the ministry took shape in his mind. He was encouraged by example as well as inclination. One of his professors, Lewis Sperry Chafer, was at the time an instructor in music. Calvitt, more mature than the other students because of his days in the business world, was often treated more like an equal by the instructors. Chafer confided in the lad one day, "Calvitt, I have been studying the Bible a great deal recently and have been asked to lecture in a number of churches. I believe I am going to make this my life's work." Professor Chafer was as good as his word. Soon thereafter he left the Mount Hermon campus and turned to Bible teaching in many places throughout the country. Eventually, he settled in Texas where he founded the Dallas Theological Seminary and where, too, he produced at least two dozen books on theology and the Bible.

Leaving Mount Hermon, Calvitt still had a few hours of preparatory education to complete. Unsure of his next step, he called on his pastor, Dr. S. Parkes Cadman. The servant who opened the door of the big brownstone manse (just a few doors away from "that barn of an iron-ceilinged church" known as Central Congregational) took Calvitt's name to Dr. Cadman. That illustrious man, the servant carefully explained, was busy in his study on "next Sunday's sermon." Calvitt remembered with awe that Dr. Cadman had once told his mother, "I always write out my sermons. It is the discipline of the pen!"

Ushered into his presence, Calvitt was startled to find the good man smoking a pipe. "Smoking in those days," he reminisces, "was pretty much a monopoly of the Episcopalian clergy. He also wore a clerical collar and as I recall that, too, was considered pretty 'high church.' But I was always deeply impressed by his looks and by his ability. He was, to my mind, one of the finest ministers America has ever produced." On that particular occasion, busy as he was, he received Calvitt with warm cordiality. Although he had not seen the lad in several years, he remembered many details about him and asked about every member of the family. "Then, almost abruptly," Calvitt Clarke recalled in later years, "his tone changed. My heart sank as he pointed his finger at me and asked, 'What is this I've heard about your wanting to be a preacher?' Fortunately, I detected a twinkle in his eye as he continued, 'Have you no ambition? Don't you want to get rich—own a yacht—take it easy—sail to the South Seas?'"

Catching his mood, Calvitt replied, "If I owned a yacht, I'd get caught in a typhoon—and then I'd drown. I'd better be a preacher."

"The smile that lit his face made me feel good all over," he remembers. "That was a man who cared about people— even about a boy who had interrupted him in his work. There was a basic human quality in his smile that seemed to reveal all of the hopes and dreams he had ever had. But better than that, for a young lad in his teens, it had the electric quality of assuring me my own hopes and dreams could come true!"

As he listened to Calvitt's problems, he said, "I think I have just the place for you." Getting up from his chair, he went to the foot of the stairs. Raising his rich preacher's voice to its best resonance, he called, "Mother, what was the name of that college Cornelius Wolfkin was telling us about?" The answer came: "Denison University, Granville, Ohio."

Dr. Cadman put his hand on the boy's shoulder on his way back to the room. "Women remember things, Calvitt," he philosophized, "and they are very wise people. Incidentally, Denison is Baptist and we are Congregationalists. Does that worry you, my boy?" Calvitt shook his head. "Good," said the minister. "Remember, God's children are under many roofs." So Calvitt went to Denison.

As he remembers it, "In Denison I was no bookworm. I was only good in those subjects that did not require study.

I surely did not shine in Latin, Greek or mathematics. In English and history, however, I did do quite a bit better. There was a popular saying on the campus, 'Never let your studies interfere with your social life.' I guess it has gained universal popularity since then. I am sorry to say that it had some appeal for me, for I spent many happy and carefree days in the pretty little town of Granville."

Whatever his scholastic attainment at Denison, the college paper did a profile on him in his senior year, using for the first time the nickname "Champ" which has followed him ever since. "Champ," said the article, "while here at Denison has been first in war, first in peace and first in the hearts of his college mates." Beginning to open out, Calvitt Clarke's personality was developing a warmth that would win him thousands of friends throughout the world.

The next step was attending theological seminary in Pittsburgh. Calvitt undertook many other activities there as well. "I was busier," he said, "than a hen with a brood of ducklings at the edge of a pond!" Beside the regular seminary course, he studied for an M.A. at Washington and Jefferson College, was pastor of two Presbyterian churches, organized many county committees for Near East Relief, managed to squeeze in some writing (one article appearing in the old *Presbyterian Banner*), and even made some speeches on behalf of Woman's Suffrage. At the same time he was frequently seen in neighborhood theatres and on Pittsburgh street corners as one of the "Four-Minute-Men" for the war effort. World War I was then in progress and the Government was attempting to awaken the citizenry to coming emergencies.

This exhausting activity began to take its toll. "One night," he says, "I went to sleep on a platform before the eyes of 2,000 people. My fellow-speaker must have had a particularly soothing voice. To employ a cliché, it was life's most embarrassing moment!"

Despite all this pellmell activity, however, Calvitt, found time for a decision that was to prove the most vital one of his life. While preaching in his accustomed "student pulpit" one Sunday morning, he noticed a stranger coming down the aisle, a very beautiful stranger. "At that moment" he says now, "I thought to myself, 'I will never doubt miracles again for I am being visited by a blond angel'!" After the service, he greeted the parishioners, but as Helen Caroline Mattson was afterward to testify, "He did not shake my hand. He squeezed it!" The record also indicates that he asked for a date "that very night." On the following night during a second date he proposed to her. Neither can remember whether she said "yes" on that evening. An outside observer might have commented that she was stunned! It is fairly evident, however, that she did not discourage him too greatly. Shortly after that, on a snowy December day in 1913, he and Helen said "I do" to some propositions that have been satisfactorily realized ever since. As his associate and companion, Mrs. Helen Clarke has truly been his "other self."

Over his desk hangs a motto given him years ago by a friend, "The road to success is filled with men being pushed by their wives." His eyes light up with a twinkle whenever he looks at it. "It's true," he says with a smile.

In the early spring of 1918, he felt the urgent call to minister to troops overseas through the work of the YMCA. He was not due to be graduated from seminary until June of that year, but the school's administrative board, after examination of his grades, agreed to bestow his degree, Bachelor of Divinity, *in absentia*.

For the first time, he turned to helping some of the world's needy people in person.

THREE

An American In Paris
and Beyond

CALVITT CLARKE sailed aboard one of the American troop transport ships in April of 1918, leaving his beloved Helen and two babies, Jeanne and Calvitt, Jr. He had said goodbye on the East Liberty platform in Pittsburgh and as he made his way to his seat he relates that his every "impulse was to get off the train at the next station and return." Had it not been for the urgency of his YMCA mission, he "certainly would have taken the pilot boat back from Sandy Hook."

France at war was quite a shock for a young man fresh out of theological seminary. His work carried him from one end of the country to the other and exposed him to sights that were a jolt to a sensitive and comparatively sheltered theological student.

Writing later of one experience in Marseilles, he said: "It has justly been called one of the most wicked cities of the world. I remembered the first time I visited it just after the close of World War I. I had not been on the street more than five minutes when I witnessed a terrific knife fight between some sailors over a prostitute. In all these years I have never forgotten the expression on that woman's face—so cruel and evil. I felt she would have been glad if they had killed one another. Fortunately, the police stepped in before fatal injury had occurred. But there were streets and alleys I could not enter because I was in a uniform provided by the Army for YMCA workers. The Army had those streets marked 'Out of Bounds'—and well so."

Most of his labors in France were with the "stranded" Russian troops—200,000 of them—who had been held up from returning to their homeland. The Allies were fearful at the time that they might join the Bolshevik Revolution, then simmering. This would have been particularly disastrous since the Allies were then mounting a countermovement in Russia with bases in and around the city of Archangel.

Preaching to and helping these men broadened Calvitt's viewpoint and his awareness. He later admitted some weaknesses in the YMCA approach of those days. His defense of the "Y," however, and of its activities during World War I is forthright: "The truth is, the YMCA had more helpful activities than all the other war agencies combined!" He frequently recalled a friend who complained bitterly about the "miserable work of the 'Y'" during the war. Then switching to another gripe, the friend complained of the manner in which Army cooks "spoiled perfectly good food." Apparently forgetting his original premise, he then said, "I tell you, Calvitt, if it hadn't been for the cookies and hot chocolate they gave me at the 'Y,' I would have starved to death."

When the YMCA closed down its overseas operations for the troops, Calvitt returned home. Now, however, a new vision was suspended before his eyes. Immediately on landing, he went to the office of his friend and mentor, Dr. Stanley A. Hunter, who at that time was pastor of the North Presbyterian Church in Pittsburgh. This place of worship was then known as "The Seminary's Church." He told Dr. Hunter he was back and "looking for a church."

"I'll certainly be happy to help you," Stanley Hunter assured him, "but what are your plans for eating in the meanwhile—you and your family?" As it was quickly evident there were no such plans, the older man had a flash of inspiration, "Calvitt," he said, "you did a great deal of volunteer work for Armenian and Syrian relief before going to France. Why don't you try some more organizing activities for us—I'm Near East Relief's regional secretary here—until you find a church." Calvitt gladly agreed, and was soon employed by Near East Relief. He remained with that organization until it was dissolved in the mid-thirties. He never did find that church.

His work began in Harrisburg, where he was appointed Director for Central Pennsylvania. One conversation with that charity's Treasurer, William Jennings, remained fresh in his mind for years afterward. Jennings, then in his prime, was a wise and kindly gentleman with a shrewdness that had elevated him to the presidency of the Commonwealth Bank and Trust Company. One day, however, he gave Calvitt some advice that was to prove adversely prophetic. "Clarke," he said, "you should be looking for some other kind of work. The war is over, and there will not always be hungry children for whom you can raise money. Sooner or later you will just run out of needy youngsters!" Meditating on those words years later, Calvitt Clarke said laconically, "The supply of needy youngsters has always been abundant."

Slowly he rose to executive status in this important charity. Speaking in Pennsylvania churches and later in all parts of the country, he often raised amounts averaging $1,000 per speech for the cause. His persuasive powers were beginning to pay dividends. Another aspect of the work at which he became particularly proficient was the organization of clothing drives in various communities.

Probably the largest single collection of used clothing ever assembled took place on a spring day in 1925. The place was Philadelphia—the organizer was J. Calvitt Clarke who by now had risen to the office of Assistant Regional Director for the Middle Atlantic States. The year previously, there had been a one-day-collection in which the police and fire stations had been employed as "Bundle Stations." The collection had been a success, most of the clothing being brought from their homes by school children. However, when similar plans for a city-wide, one-day-collection were laid for 1925, the city authorities passed an ordinance forbidding the use of police and fire stations.

A hasty conference was called at which all the Philadelphia Near East Relief staff was present. It looked as though the thousands of pounds of clothing desperately needed by adults and children in Armenia and Syria would be lost. It was at this moment that an organizing inspiration came to Dr. Clarke. The words that he spoke at that meeting laid the foundation for the collection of millions of dollars of used clothing in later years, not only to Armenians but to shivering children all over the world. His words were simple and direct; "If school children have been our real collectors up to now, why should they bring the clothing to police and fire stations anyway? Why can't they just bring it to school? Let's make it a public and parochial school campaign!"

The idea was an immediate success. The superintendent of Philadelphia's public schools, as well as the Catholic Bishop, gave their enthusiastic approval. "It was as though a dam had burst!" said Calvitt Clarke. Others, too, quickly lent their aid. The department stores arranged for their trucks, after the day's final delivery, to pick up clothing. But though this arrangement was carefully mapped out, it was discovered that even such a fleet of trucks was insufficient. Volunteer telephone operators went to work calling wholesale houses to enlist additional transportation. The Pennsylvania Railroad donated many of its freight cars for direct service to the New York docks.

"When I visited the Pennsylvania freight yards," said Dr. Clarke many years later, "it was the most active scene I have ever beheld. The trucks came into the yard in long lines, bumper-to-bumper. Load after load was rapidly being thrown from vehicles of every description into the open doors of the railroad cars. I even saw some police patrol wagons and city policemen who had been caught up in the enthusiasm. It was magnificent!"

As he visited in Armenia from time to time he was to see the fruit of this marvelous cooperation. "I stopped in the then-locked-up cities such as Tiflis, where Stalin was born. There I saw children and adults by the thousands, wearing clothes that had once been on the counters of Wanamaker's, Gimbel's, and other Philadelphia stores." What a thrill it must have been for a young man to see the tangible results of his own inspiration!

All, of course, was not "peaches and cream" in his endeavors. Occasionally, he faced a few "spinach" experiences. He recalled one instance when he attempted to collect clothing in a small town. Summoned to the office of the Director of Social Welfare, he faced a glowering enemy of overseas relief. "I could put you in jail for soliciting in Pennsylvania without a license!," blustered the Director. Calvitt promptly presented the license in question and then, out of curiosity, asked, "Surely, you wouldn't put a person in jail for helping poor people?" With evident pride, the Director snapped back, "I have one man cooling his heels in jail right now!"

These difficulties had a way of smoothing out, however. The next year when Dr. Clarke returned to the same town, the Director had been replaced by a man who was as friendly as the other had been inimical. He went the "second mile" by introducing Calvitt to a paper-collecting firm. Two fine men who were brothers ran this company. They collected the clothing in their own trucks, baled it, and put it on the freight cars. Total cost to Near East Relief: Dr. Clarke's grateful thanks.

It was in the early twenties that Near East Relief first sent this able young man to Armenia to observe the actual work and to ascertain its needs. In one of his monthly letters not long ago, Dr. Clarke recalled this first trip to the Middle East. "Trying to straighten up a desk the other day, I found a little bottle I had brought home from Armenia in the 1920's. Still in it was a mixture of dried grasshoppers and pounded tree bark. On this food alone thousands of Armenians were trying to escape death by starvation.

"One who has never witnessed a famine cannot imagine the horror of my journey around Mt. Ararat, in the Russian Caucasus, and down almost to the Iranian border: Little children with legs like pipestems and stomachs bloated and swollen by just such food; children lying or sitting on the ground so weak from hunger that they made no effort to brush away the flies that crawled over their eyeballs; the dead lying in the streets."

Deep spiritual impressions—in faith as well as in charity—were left on him during this same era. Writing of his travels through Palestine in 1924 he said, "One cannot walk the streets of Nazareth without a deep feeling of reverence. Here is an old carpenter shop such as He would have worked in—here, the same roughly paved streets He must have walked. Some of these same houses He must have seen. Perhaps He leaned against this very wall that you, hesitantly, with a mumbled prayer, dare lean against yourself. And you think of Him who was a boy here, or later, taking children into His arms and saying 'Of such is the kingdom of heaven!' "

In his mind's eye, as he wrote, he must have seen the picture of those children with "pipestem legs"—too weak to brush away the flies. It may have been then that he first heard the weeping of the children of the world. Certain it is that the sights of those early journeys—the children huddled in the culverts and gutters; children with parched tongues and cracked lips; children too weary to cry out—left an indelible mark on his heart.

Laboring long days and nights throughout the twenties and thirties, Calvitt Clarke and his family were constantly on the move, pleading, begging, persuading. He was, successively, Director of Near East Relief's Ohio area, Director for Minnesota and the Dakotas, and finally Regional Director for the entire southeastern United States. It was at this time that he established his personal residence in Richmond, Virginia, where he has remained ever since.

In the middle of the 1930's the need for emergency relief to the Armenians largely ceased. With it, Near East Relief as an organization came to an end. Several exceedingly needy causes presented themselves to him at this time. He became, from 1931 to 1933, National Secretary and Southern Director of the Golden Rule Foundation, an agency dedicated to the fostering of Christian principles in sharing. He also worked for a while with the National Foundation for the Blind. During the years 1937 to 1938, he arranged many lectures for Helen Keller.

But Calvitt Clarke's heart was more and more called to the needs of hungry, abandoned children. It was this dedication that impelled him, along with his friends Dr. John Voris and Dr. J. Stewart Nagle, to found *Save the Children Federation*, a charity still successfully in existence. Dr. Clarke always, however, gave primary credit to Dr. Voris as principal founder. From 1934 to 1937 he was Southern Director for that organization.

The time had drawn near, however, for him to respond to his life's greatest call—the care of children in China and beyond.

FOUR

Hear the Weeping of the Children

IN JULY of 1937, the guns and Zeros of Japan's Kwangtung Army attacked Chinese forces west of Peiping. The fighting and bombardment rose to fever pitch and it is estimated that between 1,000,000 and 2,000,000 children died in that vast land within the next three years. During that time, Japan seized most of China's ports and railways. The Kuomintang Government of Chiang Kai-Shek retreated first to Hankow and then to Chungking, while the Japanese set up a puppet government at Nanking.

As a result of this death struggle, the bodies of little children were strewn along the road from Tientsin to Peiping, while little living skeletons held out shriveled claws for a few grains of rice. Missionaries and relief workers saw living babies strapped to the backs of dead mothers, or lying in ditches beside the road. One missionary found a weeping and bloody infant thus strapped to her dead mother's back. Upon closer examination he found that the mother had been blasted by a bomb and killed instantly. The baby's arm had been blown off and she was quickly bleeding to death. Acting with dispatch, the missionary unstrapped the youngster, tightly bound the little stump of remaining arm, and carried the child into the nearby city. Eventually, this youngster was to grow up in one of the orphanages later established by Calvitt Clarke.

It was in the following year, 1938, that Dr. Clarke and Dr. J. Stewart Nagle met in far-off Chambersburg, Pennsylvania. News of the skeleton children of China had reached America and there was mounting concern. Millions were starving at that very moment. Thousands more had fled to other Eastern countries and a great colony of Chinese had settled in Singapore. Dr. Nagle, no longer with Save the Children Federation, had at one time been a Methodist missionary, and had established a boys' school in that city for homeless Chinese youngsters who had lost their parents. There had been through the years other isolated efforts of this sort. But the Sino-Japanese War hit with such sudden ferocity that Americans were generally unprepared to help.

Greatly disturbed by this untold suffering, as they walked and talked Calvitt Clarke asked the rhetorical question, "Do you feel that Americans are doing all they can to help?" The two men stood in silence gazing into a barbershop on Chambersburg's Main Street. After a moment of thought, Dr. Nagle said quietly, "You have been a money-raiser for twenty-five years. Why don't *you* do something about it?" Squaring his jaw, Dr. Clarke replied, "All right, I will."

It was at this point in time that China's Children Fund, later to be known as Christian Children's Fund, was born. Ever after Calvitt Clarke was to declare with amazed amusement that, "CCF was born in 1938, outside a barbershop in Chambersburg, Pennsylvania!"

Returning to Richmond the same day, he set to work. "A month later," he relates, "the first check went out to an orphanage in Shiu Chow, Kwangtung Province. It was a run-down Home but had the room to accommodate several hundred starving refugee children. I had to advance the first money for the postage. I visited a neighboring letter-shop owner and a printer, both of whom knew me, and told them I would be personally responsible for all bills incurred. I also called on some of my neighbors that first night and persuaded them to become committee members. Two of them still head CCF's Board—T. Nelson Parker as President, and John J. Fairbank as Vice-President. CCF was also incorporated in that year and its first office was rented in the old Richmond Trust Building on Richmond's Main Street. From that start, twenty-three years ago, in a tiny office, with two second-hand desks bought from the janitor, Christian Children's Fund has grown into the largest Protestant orphanage organization in the world, now caring for over 36,000 children in forty-eight countries around the world!"

The work in China during the late thirties and early forties was staggering. Between 10,000,000 and 15,000,000 youngsters were left homeless during the struggle and famine. Their fathers had left home to serve their country. In many instances, their mothers had been killed before the children's eyes, by machine-gunning or bombing. Others had become separated from their families during the terrible confusion and in the endless refugee lines that stretched for thousands of miles outside China's major cities.

In the thick of it all was a young missionary named Verent Mills, later to become CCF's International Coordinator. He tells of the great need for bandages and drugs in those days. "Medical supplies," he says, "were particularly scarce, especially in the southern provinces. When the Japanese captured Canton, all of the medicines of the Kwangtung International Red Cross were stored in the godowns of the Shameen (the International Settlement). At the time the Japanese Army held a line to the west of Canton from Kong Tsuen on the railroad across to Pak Naai where it followed a little river clear to Kunyin.

"It was one starless night that I crossed 'no man's land' and forded the river where I passed through the Japanese lines. Fortunately, it was dark enough so that I avoided interception by sentries. Once behind the lines, I stayed with a friendly Chinese family who were glad to hide me. While there, I learned that one of my former language teachers was now a major in the 'puppet' army. I took courage in my hands, made contact with him and explained my mission. I told him of the wounded and dying millions who needed medical aid so badly. His eyes lit up affectionately as he realized what I was trying to do.

"I will never forget how he stowed me away in the damp bottom of a sampan and had me rowed into Canton. The next day I set to work. From morning to night, day after day, parcels left the Shameen godown (warehouse) tucked under my jacket or inside my pockets. Sometimes I bulged so that I looked like Santa Claus. Inside the packages were drugs of every description which I took to the waterfront and hid in a small fleet of sampans that was forming under one of the wharfs.

"When we were fully loaded we waited for another dark night. Then with muffled oars our tiny armada toiled upriver to within seven miles of the front lines. Here we repacked our load in bamboo baskets and hoisted it onto yo-yo poles over the shoulders of faithful Chinese friends. With the help of our 'major,' our caravan passed through the front lines at a pre-arranged signal. Hundreds of lives were saved with this timely shipment."

But not all were so lucky. The tragedies continued to mount. Even those proportionately few children (several hundred thousand) who could be helped through American agencies bore traumatic impressions that they could never eradicate. "Most of their eyes were filled with tragedy," reports a newspaper article of the time, "tragedy they could not understand. Why did fire and death rain from the skies, burning their homes and silencing forever their little brothers and sisters. . . . Why were fathers killed by intruding strangers. . . . Why were mothers spirited away so that they were never seen again?

"Memories of the hurried scurrying away from other impending terrors—following the neighbors, following people, following anybody who fled—on and on, until the act of walking seemed to be the only act of life. The gnawing pangs of hunger . . .

"Airplanes overhead again . . . the shrieking swoop as they bear down on the refugee lines. . . . See, this little girl has lost her teeth when she fell running from a swooping plane. These two little boys and their fathers gave the last places in the boat to their mothers and little sisters so that they might escape to the other side of the river. The boat never came back again.

"Stealthily, in the darkness, the fathers and the little sons fashioned a crude craft of bamboo and before darkness had lifted, made their way across, too. But the fear-driven refugees had swept on, and no amount of searching ever brought such little families together again.

"Here is a small girl who has been wandering so long that she does not remember much about her family or home. Here, too, is a beautiful child from a cultured home. There are thousands of others from every background."

How to help these youngsters! This was the problem faced by Calvitt Clarke—how to establish a relationship between the children and American friends so that their young lives would be protected and their futures assured. In these moments of quandary, Dr. Clarke reached back into his experience as co-founder of Save the Children Federation and introduced his concept of the "Adoption Plan." Quickly he began to cement the relationship between a child overseas and his "foster parent" in America. The miracle of human love prevailed, even in a world torn with hatred and chaos. Miles away across the Pacific were "un-ugly" Americans who, following the guidance of J. Calvitt Clarke, cared and cared terribly about every one of these little children. Each such American who responded to Dr. Clarke's pleas received the picture of a child to whom he began to write as well as to send packages and help. There were no legal ties, of course, for "adoption" was just a term used for convenience, but sponsors soon began to refer to these Chinese babies on the other side of the world as "my little son" and "my little daughter." One sponsor wrote in those early days, "I would like Mei Chan to call me Aunt Mary. I want to observe her birthday every year. What do you suppose she would like for her birthday this year?"

These friendly Americans began to multiply by the tens, the hundreds, and finally, by the thousands. They responded from every walk of life. An outstanding poet, an internationally known club woman, the head of a nationwide children's theatre, a big-league baseball player and his family, the heads of faculty members of many schools and colleges, a lady in Hawaii, a fraternity in Puerto Rico, office staffs, student groups, little children who sent their savings from piggy-banks, kind rich people and kind poor people, business men and housewives—these were a cross-section of America that "adopted" Chinese children.

CCF personnel paid the price, too. In 1944, the work in China with its special complications had reached such proportion that Dr. Clarke felt someone especially responsible should be in the field. After consulting with the Board, he therefore appointed Mr. Erwin Raetz to the position of General Superintendent in Charge of China Orphanages. The journey during the war was hazardous in the extreme. It was necessary for Mr. Raetz' ship to pick up convoys going the long way around since the Pacific bristled with Japanese ships and submarines. Sailing from New York in the late spring of 1944, he took what supplies he could, for communication was difficult to maintain. He told the story of his trip to his wife in a letter dated January 1945:

"We left Suez for Bombay, the last part of our long journey on July 21. One of the passengers was an elderly lady of 82 years, returning to India to join her husband, a captain in the British army. She had a number of heart attacks before we reached Karachi, and the ship's doctor did not think she would live to see India. I did my best to look after her and as it was hard for her to breathe inside the ship, she spent most of her time on deck. It was very warm so I spent most of my time on deck usually retiring about midnight.

"On Saturday night, it seemed I had hardly been asleep when I was awakened by a dull thud. Dazed, I put on the lights to assemble a few things, when it went out. Then I smelled smoke and things began falling all around me. I dropped everything, grabbed my life-jacket and rushed up to the deck in the dark to the life-boat station where I had been assigned. I did not see a soul. After a few moments I looked up and found that the boat was gone—it had been blown to bits. Just then the elderly lady appeared. I caught her by the arm and took her around the deck looking for another life-boat—but in vain.

"Suddenly she sank down on a chair with another heart attack. She told me, 'I can't go any further—you go without me.' My first thought was to stay with her and try to get her off somehow. She refused a life-jacket and she was too large a woman for me to lift into a life-boat. I thought of her age and poor health. I remembered, too, that I had a family in America and work to do in China. By now water was flooding the deck. I knew we would both be lost if I waited much longer. Suddenly a huge wave swept over the deck taking me off my feet. For a few seconds I did not know whether I was on or off the ship. But I do remember talking with God.

"I said, 'Lord, are you going to take me home this way? I am in Thy hands—Thy will be done.' When the wave receded I found myself still on the ship. I caught sight of a raft which I thought I had better cling to before I was washed away again so I climbed aboard. Two Indian passengers, seeing me, hopped on too. I suddenly realized that it would never hold three of us, so I got off and so did they. One of them walked down the deck and cried, 'I'm lost! I'm lost!' I was just about to cast myself into the sea (as others were doing, hoping to be rescued) when I saw a member of our gun crew leading a woman passenger who was hysterical. I made toward them and caught sight of a life-boat just being lowered. Just as it was even with the rail I jumped in one end and they in the other. It was filled with the frightened Indian crew-members. They should have been lowering the boat rather than the British officers who had taken over the job. I got busy passing the ropes of the life-boat and began to think there would never be an end to them. Just as we got clear of the ropes a huge wave carried us up in the air and it looked as though we would be crushed against the side of the ship. I prayed out loud, just one sentence, 'God, get us out of this.' He heard.

"We collided with other life-boats and at times I thought we would certainly smash each other to pieces. In this, too, the Lord looked after us and we finally drifted apart. It began to rain and turned cold. We were packed in like sardines and the waves were so high that we all became very sick. Our boat was leaking badly, as the plug had been knocked out when we struck the water. But the engineers, sick as they were, got the hand-pump working and kept the boat bailed out. Suddenly, we were told by an officer 'put the little red lights on your jackets out! There is a ship coming!'

"Suspecting it to be a sub coming to strafe us, all the Indians began to pray to Allah. It turned out to be a British corvette cruising around looking for us. After throwing a number of lines to us, we finally caught one and they pulled us along-side. But getting aboard was no easy job. Each of us had to stand at the bow of the life-boat, and as the waves lifted us even with the corvette, we jumped for the deck.

"The railing was lined with sailors who grabbed us and helped us onto the ship. With so many survivors on such a small vessel we looked like flies all over the deck. Water was rationed and food was scarce, but the officers and crew did everything they could to make us comfortable. In two days, we were back in Karachi and were taken aboard another ship into the harbor. The British Red Cross gave us overnight kits and the next day we were taken to the American Red Cross where we were fitted with clothing. They also gave us our first good meal in some time and generally treated us very well.

"I was quite fit after landing in Karachi but I must admit that I didn't feel too good about returning to Bombay over the same route. Well, the Lord brought me through all that and here I am in China."

Mr. Raetz established regional headquarters in Canton and began picking up scores of children from the highways and bringing them to the CCF's forty-odd homes. In his position as China Director, he remained as an important member of China's Children Fund until 1950 when he went into missionary work of a more specific nature.

As the years of Japanese invasion continued, the severity of the conditions stepped up. Rape, murder and banditry followed in the wake of each new incursion. China, with her 450,000,000 people, her vast coal, iron, tung oil and antimony, holed up in the inland mountains. Although she suffered dreadfully in those days, she fought back, slaying two million Japanese soldiers and holding a million more at bay. But the cost to the economy in natural resources, commerce and lives was overwhelming. And the children continued to starve by the millions. An eye-witness of that era said, "I heard the begging children in shrill cries, or nearer death in gaping whispers, 'I'm hungry, so hungry—please help me!' Even the trees cried out in the famine. They stood stripped and naked, their bark torn from them to make soup. All of the animals were eaten long ago, except a few dogs, once pets, now wild, driven mad with hunger. Hunger! most horrible of all war's outrages!"

In 1943, reports like the following came through to CCF headquarters in Richmond: "China has paid a terrific price. Five million Chinese lives have been snuffed out. Fifty million more have been made homeless, and more than two million children have become orphans. Famine conditions exist in every province with hundreds of thousands dead from starvation. Inflation has multiplied the cost of rice ten or twelve times in as many months. A single aspirin tablet costs $2.70, while a gallon of gasoline costs $180. All of China's principal cities are in the hands of the enemy, nine-tenths of her industries are destroyed or captured, and her communication with the outside world is practically closed except for a mere trickle over mountain passes or by a dozen or so cargo planes . . . Only the most stalwart people continue to fight when their blood runs in rivers and their dead pile in hills!"

CCF's workers and orphanages were, of course, suffering dreadfully by now. In South China, as well as in the north, the children were not getting enough to eat because of the Japanese blockade. Dr. Clarke was deeply disturbed over his beleaguered youngsters. One of the reports coming to him said: "Things are getting more serious for us every day. Foods are getting scarcer and scarcer. No one ever feels satisfied after eating, especially the children. They are always hungry. I have sold all my jewelry, my silverware, my radio. I don't know what will be the next to go. I have lost forty-six pounds since the war broke out. A lot of people don't recognize me now when they see me on the streets."

But the savagery continued and the privation. Cut off from

their families in Japan, the soldiery of that country followed policies that the military has pursued in every age. "In one city," said another report, "the Japanese massacred 2,300 men and raped 5,090 women, of whom 164 died. They kidnapped 181 women to be used as camp prostitutes and took along 3,400 able-bodied men and 320 children to be camp workers and slaves."

One eye-witness said, "I saw a soldier raping a woman on the open street. When her baby, lying on the ground beside her, started to cry, the soldier reached over and smothered it with his coat."

The United States State Department estimated that at least 200,000 illegitimate children of mixed-blood were fostered in this way. Chinese girls of six and seven were no more exempt from this type of treatment than were grandmothers of fifty or sixty.

Despite the lawlessness, which seemed officially planned by the enemy military, there were many instances of kindness shown by individual Japanese officers and soldiers. There were occasions when these men, unwatched by their superiors, would bring food to the youngsters in CCF Homes. In more than one instance, a ragged child would be brought to an orphanage door because of the compassion of a Nipponese infanytryman. There were frequently rays of light, such as this one, that shone into the darkness of the savage war.

Soon, however, as though the ancient gods were angry, nature, too, turned on the hard-pressed Chinese. Droughts and floods hit widely separated areas. The spirit of the people sank lower than ever before, and again the children were the greatest sufferers.

An orphanage superintendent, writing from Central China said, "The restlessness has subdued somewhat. When conditions first became bad, men, women and children, families and whole villages were constantly moving on and on in search of food and better conditions. But the famine swathe is wide. Now hunger has weakened and slowed them down. Many of them have ceased their endless, dogged walking. They sit and wait to die—all of them including the children. I hate to see people giving up, but what can they do? The countryside is stripped of everything that could give a bit of nourishment."

In the mid-forties, Reverend Verent Mills was still laboring in South China. Although he was still conducting relief work to aid the thousands of refugees, he had now also "adopted" 142 orphans whom he had gathered from the straggling hundreds that daily passed through his makeshift camp. This had been literally thrown up to provide a meal of rice or a night's rest to the hordes of weary folk before they continued on the rugged trek inland.

The children he had gathered were survivors of the Japanese invasion of Canton and Sz Yup who had been too tiny or too weak to keep up the pace. Mills and his little family of orphans had moved slowly overland before the advancing troops. When they finally arrived at Shin Hing Gorge on the West River, they felt they were safe for the moment. Here Mills set up another of his many soup kitchens to feed his youngsters and the burdened refugees who were pouring past.

Their sojourn here was not for long, however. A few nights later, in the blackness of the night, artillery shells began to burst all around. The Japanese were on their heels again. The children awakened, terrified. Many of them screamed while others, too terrified, simply trembled. Quickly Mills gathered his handful of faithful helpers and like the other refugees, took to the rocky road. Over his shoulder rested a bamboo pole with an infant in a basket suspended at either end. The other children, many not more than toddlers, trailed along with him as best they could—some in front, others behind, like a hen with her chicks. They struggled through the darkness, not venturing to light a lantern since a light would surely have drawn enemy gunfire. Many of the children stumbled and fell. "There were many stubbed toes and bloody knees," reminisced Mills, "but the little group pressed on, often just feeling their way over the stony mountain pass." Laden as he was with the baskets, Mills began to sing. Before long the children joined in the chorus, too. "A simple song, a smile, a pat on the head," he said, "seemed miraculously to boost their morale and keep them going."

"Another six long weary weeks went by," he relates. "We had no bathing facilities, no laundry. We were covered with lice—every one of us. As we scratched our way over hill and dale, I pondered the phrase 'China's millions.' At the moment it seemed as though they were living on us! Day after day, down the dusty road, up and down the mountain slopes—some days only making a few miles—at long last we arrived in Shiu Chow. A motley, sorry-looking crowd we were!"

No one knew they were coming. They marched as best they could up to the gate of Po Kong Orphanage. It was the first orphanage that Dr. Clarke had started to help when China's Children Fund was founded. Leaving his children in the street, he went in to see the superintendent. "I have 142 homeless children," he told the startled man, "can you take us in?" When the superintendent went into the street and saw the youngsters in their misery, he said, "How can I turn you away?"

With his children safely ensconced at Po Kong, Mills was soon on his way. He retraced his steps to the famine area in Sz Yup. Time was pressing urgently, for hundreds were dying. Covering 460 miles in twelve days he was soon in the distressed area again.

After the long hike he finally arrived in Sam Fau where he found he could avail himself of boat travel and save himself further steps. In relating his experience to me he said, "I was dog-tired, so I put up in a little Chinese inn. I had no sooner

lain down for the night, when an over-powering odor of decay
smote my nostrils. Looking out the window, I discerned in
the faint light what looked like hundreds of logs piled high
in the inn's back courtyard. The next morning I saw to my
dismay that these 'logs' were, in truth, the rotting bodies of
famine victims stacked like cord-wood in and around the inn.
People were dying so fast it was impossible to keep up with
the burial.

"I have never seen anything like it, before or since," he
recalled with a shudder, "not even in India where famines
are so bad. As I went farther south through the Toishan
district, I saw the famine-dead with their bloated stomachs
everywhere I looked."

But this was only the beginning for Mills, as he remained in
the Sz Yup area for over two years. There he organized a Relief Committee and opened twenty-one soup kitchens that
eventually fed 45,000 starving people daily. In addition, he
"adopted" 700 more orphan children for whom he constructed
five makeshift homes.

With ever-increasing needs of this sort, many missions and
orphanages wrote to Dr. Clarke asking for help from China's
Children Fund. And, of course, as funds became available,
more and more Homes were added to CCF's growing network
of orphanages. The calls for aid were often pathetic and were
couched in poignant words. Superintendent Paulson of the
Lutheran-CCF Orphanage in Kwangtung wrote in early 1943,
"After we had taken nine more strayed orphans into our
home, our Mission asked us to stop because it would become
impossible to help more. We had to be very heartless against
so many children crying for pity out of a bundle of rags at our
door. I cannot sleep at night for thinking of those dying children whom I have had to refuse to help. I have the buildings
and the Chinese workers who love children, and yet they are

starving and left to die. If there were only the funds to help them!"

In the face of pleas such as these, Dr. and Mrs. Clarke redoubled their efforts for the children. The Homes, however, were facing troubles that they had never envisioned before. That ever-recurring evil of opium began rearing its head and affected many homes, and the lives of many children. In an effort to demoralize the populace, the farmers of southern Shansi Province were required to grow poppies, the seeds of which could be obtained free of charge from the Special Services of the occupying army. A farmer who possessed thirty mow of land was forced to plant ten mow; if he had less than that, he had to plant at least five in poppies.

In the light of recent USIS reports, a concerted policy of the Red Chinese Government is now following similar lines. Southwest China is at present devoting much of its acreage to the growth of poppies for the international opium traffic. This flows largely unhindered through Thailand, as well as other distribution points, and even with stringent controls in Hong Kong and Macao the dope is smuggled through. At present this evil traffic is being used to demoralize the youth of our western nations.

A description of raids near CCF's Po Kong Industrial Home in Shiu Chow is still extant from letters "flown over the Japanese lines." "Many new children," says the dispatch, "are being added to the Po Kong family during these recent months, for the Japanese have again made invasion raids very close by. In fact, in the town of Shiu Chow, five hundred homes and places of business have just been destroyed and thousands have been left homeless, without clothing or possessions, except what they have on their backs."

With Pearl Harbor in 1941, it had become impossible, of course, for Americans to negotiate with the Japanese in order to get help to the Homes. Communications were virtually cut off. Many letters never reached CCF's sponsors and friends and more circuitous routes of communication had to be established. Yet despite these multiplying problems, China's Children Fund steadily increased its work, until by 1944, it was helping forty-five orphanages in mainland China.

Privations and circumstances steadily worsened for every Home. Rations for the youngsters were cut from a meagre half-pound of rice to a mere three ounces. In addition, the superintendents, uneasy because of inevitable wartime immorality, made every effort to move their girls inland to Free China. This was a long hard trip for the girls, many of them still very tiny, and all of them greatly weakened by wartime privations. But slowly the transfer trek was made to the inland Homes.

Unfortunately, however, this did not remove the children from all harm. Several of the orphanages were so badly battered by bombs that they had to be abandoned. One of CCF's Kunming orphanages was virtually destroyed and many children killed or injured. Only funds provided in the nick of time, brought in over the Burma Road, kept the doors open to provide vital succor to the children.

The migration of many of CCF's children was accomplished at the time by the simultaneous migration of 50,000,000 Chinese refugees (at the time this was a number greater than the entire population of France). It proved to be the greatest mass trek in history. Millions died on the journey, the majority dropping by the wayside from exhaustion and hunger. Among these, of course, were many world-weary babies and children.

When the Pacific War finally came to a close on V-J Day in 1945, the orphanages of CCF were able to consolidate some of their gains and to survey the field. With the cessation of hostilities, Dr. Clarke and his many helpers were given a breathing-spell to work on rehabilitation, although this was to be short-lived before the next major catastrophe struck China.

FIVE

What They Say In Japan

WHEN "The Bomb" fell on Hiroshima, the reeling Japanese Army capitulated. Terrible hardship was everywhere and CCF again was one of the first to send aid. Dr. Clarke had been one of the first in the late '30's to sound the alarm concerning Japanese militarism. Now he moved rapidly to offer help.

In 1939 and 1940, he had warned America repeatedly that the military junta in that nation was planning war. He protested selling Japan scrap iron (including New York City's dismantled Sixth Avenue Elevated) and unlimited oil supplies. Many Americans had condemned him for his courageous stand. On November 15, 1941, a woman had written angrily, "You ought to be ashamed of yourself! The Japanese would never make war on America!" A little more than two weeks later, planes bearing the insignia of The Rising Sun were dropping what could have been the Sixth Avenue "L" on Hawaii.

However, with the signing of the 1945 Armistice on board the *U.S.S. Missouri*, in Tokyo Bay, Dr. Clarke's humanitarian heart went out to Nippon's bleeding children. Within a short time he was appealing to CCF's friends:

"There are 50,000,000 Japanese who are struggling to survive . . . and only by winning the hearts of a former enemy can

41

a peace be enduring." A missionary by the name of Miss Maud Powlas was quickly engaged by CCF to seek out orphaned youngsters in Japan and to care for them. The first of Japan's CCF's Homes was erected with these unforgettable words, "The only walls that will stand are the sheltering walls of friendship!"

Analyzing Japan's basic food needs, Dr. Clarke hastened to send funds for the children's nutrition. "There is a constant struggle," he reminded CCF's friends, "to get enough to eat. The population of Japan is more than half that of the United States, but the area of Japan is slightly less than that of California. Most disheartening of all is the fact that of this small area, only 16 per cent is really usable for crop production!"

CCF workers reported to him that there were thousands of "wild" children in Japan huddled around the railroad stations and under the bridges. Their fathers had never come back, and the mothers of many of them had perished from malnutrition or TB. Little Hirashuko was typical of these youngsters. Her father had perished in one of the raids on Okinawa. Her mother labored in a Kanagawa war factory. One day when Hirashuko was riding a street car to meet her mother at the plant, an air-raid alarm sounded. The car screeched to a halt and the occupants scattered to shelters. When Hirashuko emerged, she saw that her mother's factory was an inferno of leaping flames. She stayed beside the gutted building for days and watched the embers die out, but she never saw her mother again. Then she remembered her mother's last advice to her, "If anything should happen to me, Hirashuko, buy yourself a shoeshine kit." Desperately, she spent her last yen in this way. Somehow she managed to eke out a living by shining shoes outside Sakuragicho Station in Yokohama. At night she lived with a thousand other ragged, forsaken children in the dark and mouldy cave of a subway.

But one night some older boys stole her shoeshine box and she began to starve. She was typical of many similar youngsters found by workers and brought to a CCF Home.

The number of these children increased alarmingly, and with them came a proportionate rise in juvenile crime. Many youngsters, too, had not been orphaned but were cast off by families too poor to support them. Still others had run away from home, attracted by the excitement and glamor of adventure. Among the most pathetic, however, were the thousands of repatriated girls and boys from China and Manchuria. According to a news report of the time, "In one such group there were thirty-three children. The oldest was twelve, the youngest a baby girl of two. Only six were in good health, while eighteen were afflicted with tuberculosis resulting from malnutrition." The most tragic, however, was a six-year-old girl who descended from the train carrying four small packages which contained the ashes of her father, her mother, her brother and her baby sisters. They had all died in the final Allied attack on Kirin.

These "surplus" children appeared everywhere. They gathered on the Ginza street corners, or at the Ueno railroad station. Many of the boys and girls carried homemade shoeshine kits. Others waited to pounce on cigarette butts tossed away by G.I.'s. When enough of these had been accumulated, the children made cigarettes out of the used tobacco. Others went in for more questionable practices—in the city of Osaka, for example, one ruthless gangster gathered these children from the streets and taught them to pick pockets. With their training period finished, the graduates were often "sold" to other underworld characters. The girls of ten or twelve were soon siphoned off for the brothels of the Yoshiwara district.

Many of the children in the Osaka area were gathered up by a kindly minister named Haruka Nakamura. With the later assistance of CCF he was able to increase aid to hundreds of children clustered about the stations. Some of the stories he told me in 1960 were pathetic in the extreme. He related the story of Yoshie Ishida, a five-year-old child. "The boy," he said, "was abandoned on the cold platform at the Osaka Railroad Station on a winter night in 1946. He was brought up haphazardly by the other waifs that were living in that shelter. Even at his tender age, he was taught by them to steal, until he was soon a 'marked boy.' Eventually, the police brought him to me, because they knew I was caring for such children."

As I walked around the lovely Osaka Suije Rinkopan Home, set on the green hillside, I marveled at what had been accomplished over the years since the war. Proudly, Reverend Nakamura told me, "Last March we sent twelve children into the world. One, graduating from a barber school, began a new life as a hairdresser in town. Another got a job in an ironworks, and still another in a tailor shop. One girl started her new life as a hospital nurse. It was wonderful to see their eyes full of hope. We prayed that God would follow each of them with blessing."

This has been the story of hundreds there, rescued, fed and trained in Christian ways. One happy CCF sponsor in America, writing to her "daughter" in Osaka, said, "I feel today, dear Imataka, that I, myself, am beginning a new life. For the past eight years I have come to love you as my own flesh and blood. Remember to write to me, my dear, and tell me of all the good things that happen to you."

Americans have helped thousands of such young people in Japan and elsewhere through their "adoptions." Perhaps this important bridge of brotherhood will do more than any other alliances, treaties and ententes.

During the five years of the Allied Occupation of Japan, the United States and others attempted to attain three specific objectives: (1) to repatriate the Japanese armed forces and demobilize them; (2) to encourage and foster a democratic form of government in Japan; and (3) to encourage and, if necessary, help to finance the redevelopment of peacetime industry. General Douglas MacArthur was appointed by the President of the United States as the Supreme Commander for the Allied Powers in 1945 in order to help realize this three-fold goal. His realistic approach to Japan was based on the premise that, "As Japan goes, so will go the entire Far East."

Many church organizations set to work immediately to help in the far-reaching policy of rehabilitating Japan. Food needed to be shipped in. Colleges and hospitals needed to be re-established. Churches and schools had to be rebuilt. But, above all, the wild youngsters of the streets had to be sheltered and fed. Dr. Clarke encouraged his staff to establish the first CCF Home and to call it Jiai-no Mura (Merciful Love Village). Supervised by a local committee composed of both Americans and Japanese, the Home obtained a beautiful tract of land just outside Kumamoto. Here on a gentle southeasterly slope, with a view of the surrounding mountains, these children were provided with a climate of peace for the first time in their lives. Here, too, they received schooling, were taught useful trades and learned to cultivate their own farm.

Soon CCF was helping Japan with four such Homes for children. In addition to Jiai-no Mura, there were Bott Memorial Orphanage, Ikusei En and the Mayer Home. To supervise this growing work Dr. Clarke appointed Mr. Seiji Giga as Japanese Executive Secretary. Born in 1917, Giga had lived through many hardships in his thirty-one years. He recalls the earthquake of 1923 when his home was destroyed with thousands of others in Tokyo. "For a week," he remembers, "the skies around Tokyo and Yokohama were filled with smoke and flames. One-third of my city and the entire city of Yokohama were leveled. I can still recall the terror and the shrieks in the night. Ninety thousand died in a single day and thousands more were injured."

Growing up in Japan during the twenties and thirties was difficult. Giga's father was a Shintoist and the descendent of a Shinto priest; his mother, a devout Buddhist. It was a strict Japanese household in which the father was the head of the home in every sense of the word. When the worldwide depression of the thirties hit Japan, as it did most other nations, the Giga family (upper middle-class by Japanese standards) suffered financial reverses. The household savings dwindled to nothing and work was scarce. Reluctantly, Seiji's father told him, "I am sorry, my son, but we cannot afford to send you to high school. You will have to go to work." The blow to his pride was too great. That evening his parents found him prone on his bedroom "tatami," his face a deadly white, his breathing shallow. In alarm, they called Seiji's uncle, a doctor. The diagnosis: attempted suicide. Rushing him to the hospital, they barely saved his life.

"When I awoke," said Seiji Giga years later, "I seemed to be in the midst of a bright haze. Almost audibly I heard a voice saying to me, 'Your life has a purpose, Seiji. Find it!' I had no way of knowing which way to turn for such a purpose. That week, however, as I walked down Tokyo's Ginza, I heard singing from a Christian church. In curiosity I entered and sat near the back. As the minister, Reverend Yorichi Manabe, spoke, I felt peculiarly drawn by the voice of One who said, 'Follow me.' It was the voice of Christ, and I have followed Him ever since."

Through rugged determination, the young man put himself through high school, no mean feat in poverty-stricken Japan. He then went on to professional school for further training. The minister of the church where he had found his purpose befriended the bewildered lad and proved to be a guide and "father" through the years.

During the war, Giga was interned by the military police for his outspoken opposition to the government policies. He was freed shortly after the cessation of hostilities. Four years later he met Verent Mills, then on an inspection tour of Japan for CCF. Mills found Giga engaged in helping homeless and friendless waifs. So impressed was he with Giga's work that he petitioned Dr. Clarke to appoint him as Executive Secretary for CCF's work in Japan. Since then, many Homes have been added to the work in that nation, until today there are sixty-one orphanages under Giga's capable leadership.

The situation in Japan in 1947 was still one of desperate poverty. CCF's staff workers saw unbelievable sights. They watched the shuffling hundreds of children on the streets, with their dust-covered rags, their wild shocks of hair, their sunken eyes focused on gutters or garbage pails. One eye-witness account described the garbage pail behind the Imperial Hotel. Its contents had already been sifted by the hotel staff and by a beggars' "garbage concession." After them came a shapeless, formless pile of rags, shuffling, searching. It had a shock of matted hair and a bundle of whimpering life on its back. Perhaps it was a woman. It came every day to search through the leavings in the refuse.

On a Nara street-corner another CCF worker saw a beggar kneeling and head bent down to the sidewalk. Before this prostrate form was a tin cup and a baby bundled in rags. The bright eyes of the infant looked up at the hurrying passersby with an almost skeptical hope.

In the utter discouragement of those days, many turned to the Army of Occupation for help, both legitimate and illegitimate. From the slums of Osaka and the farms around Shirakawa came desperate girls by the tens of thousands. With the hideous privations, desperation drove more and more young girls to the Yoshiwaras of Japan. Needless to say, this situation resulted in the birth of many illegitimate children, despite the fact that abortions are legal in Japan and are performed for as little as five dollars.

In addition, due to the American Army of Occupation there were more than a few illegitimate children of mixed-blood. It is true, however, that this number was greatly exaggerated by forces inimical to America. Communist China accused American soldiers of fostering and abandoning some 200,000 such youngsters. Careful investigation proved that by February 1, 1953 there were actually 3,289 abandoned offspring of mixed parentage.

Nevertheless, there were tragic situations that broke the heart of many a modern Madame Butterfly. Yoji Takuo was one of them. A graduate of Yokohama high school in 1946, she got a job in a United States Army supply depot. There she fell in love with an American sergeant. Since at the time the Occupation rules forbade marriage, the young couple went to a nearby Shinto shrine. There they were joined in marriage by an ancient ceremony. Within a year their union was blessed with a son. His tour of duty ended, the sergeant returned to Chicago and there married another girl. His Japanese bride heartbrokenly struggled to support the son for a period of five years but eventually had to relinquish him as a public charge.

Unfortunately, there were other American boys who did not even make the overture to decency that this G.I. had made. Many of them "shacked-up" with their "only" girls, usually pick-ups from a corner bar or from the street. All too frequently their relationships resulted in illegitimate children— eventually in the several thousand illegitimate and mixed-blood children. Though more help was needed, by 1953, at least 300 of them had been cared for by Christian Children's Fund in the orphanage especially provided at the Elizabeth Saunders Home. This Home was established for this purpose by Mme. Miki Sawada, a member of one of Japan's most distinguished families.

Especial disfavor rests in the Japanese mind upon such unfortunate youngsters. I saw one such little girl—a lovely child, with a touch of blond in her curls, with blue eyes that slanted slightly at the corners. She will have a difficult time in Japan. And, yet, why should she have? The answer to this question lies in the history of that ancient nation. The Japanese have been taught that their race is unusual in that it is "pure and unmixed for over 6,000 years." The fact of the matter is that the Japanese have mixed with other oriental races many times during their history until they now include influences from China, Korea, Malaya and many other areas. Nevertheless, so deeply ingrained is the legend that the mixed-blood child is unacceptable to the average Japanese.

Added to that handicap, for little Michi-kuo of the blond tresses is the fact that she was born out of wedlock. This in itself is handicap enough. It is a well-known "secret" that one of Japan's great industrialists was a foundling who has invented a family tree to overcome this stigma.

A Westerner must realize that every aspect of living in Japan is governed by family status. If one is not a member of a family, there is no one to find you a job, no one to secure you a wife, no one to care for you in sickness. So unthinkable is this plight to the Japanese mind that there is a story of the poor school teacher, Ko Kusaba, who brooded about it night and day. He was so deeply concerned over these tots "of no family" who lived in an orphanage at the foot of Mt. Fuji that he finally decided to adopt them all. With one sweeping gesture he gave each of these youngsters his own name. To the Western ear this sounds kindly but absurd, but to the Japanese it is simply an act of great magnanimity. And today the records show 165 such children whose father is listed as Ko Kusaba.

The mixed-blood child in Japan has been taken to the heart of America, however. Such G.I. babies have been brought to America by the hundreds, in many cases accompanied by their mothers who have been reunited with their G.I. husbands. About 15,000 legal marriages have been performed between G.I.'s and Japanese brides.

While we consider this matter it is also good to know what the G.I.'s have done to establish and assist orphanages in Japan. As far north as Sapporo on the island of Hokkaido, and as far south as Nagasaki on the island of Kyushu, the American G.I. has proven his love for children by lending his muscle and money to save their lives. At the CCF Fukujuen Home outside Sapporo last year the superintendent, Mr. Kinichi Tonezawa, told me happily what the G.I.'s were doing every day. "The G.I.'s from the Chitose Air Force Base gave us a cow last week. Now we can have fresh milk for the children. They are always bringing something, or they just come to visit and play with the boys and girls!"

This sort of generosity is something that warms the American tourist's heart wherever he travels: the kindness of the G.I. to helpless children. Throughout my recent trip in the Far East, I took picture after picture of these "un-ugly" American boys holding oriental babies in their arms. One may recall, also, the many incidents in Korea such as "Operation Kiddie-Car" and "Operation Orphan Annie" which saved many young lives. These, too, are a tribute to the humanity and decency of our American G.I.'s.

Such dedication is frequently matched by the Christian concern of Japanese men and women whose hearts are drawn by the sights they saw or the wrenching experiences of the past. In 1949, the Aisenryo Home was added to CCF's growing network of orphanages. It was run by Mr. Masayasu Okayasa, who had been rescuing forlorn youngsters since V-J Day. His motivation sprang from a bitter experience which had happened to him in World War II. Every night the lights were darkened as the American planes droned overhead and the sirens announced another air raid. In those days, every Japanese house kept a large barrel of water nearby to extinguish fire bombs. During one black night his baby daughter—an only child—crawled out on the porch, fell into the barrel and was drowned. His heart was broken and nothing could console him until an inspiration came to him. "I decided," he said later, "that I would devote all I had left to helping other children." And so he began gathering them in. Indeed, "gathering them in" has been the motto of this Home ever since, as it has been the motto of the sixty other orphanages owned or assisted by CCF in Japan.

In a sense, the work of Christian Children's Fund in Japan has been, in Seiji Giga's words, "an oasis for children in the Far East." Efficient and careful, he and his staff have often provided a model for orphanages on the other side of the world.

In the spring of 1960, Dr. and Mrs. Clarke traveled to Tokyo to dedicate a new institution known as Clarke Junior College. This school is unique and marks the first of its kind in the world. It is devoted exclusively to the training of housemothers and resident staff members for Japan's CCF orphanages. Providing a complete two-year course, its college-trained faculty under its President, Rev. Takeo Nakajima, conducts classes in child welfare, educational psychology, nursing, pediatrics, social work techniques, dietetics, handwork, music and many other useful subjects. The young ladies who train here are all high school graduates who also have the opportunity for continuous field work. Their course includes the practical application of their studies through in-service care for the youngsters who live at Bott Memorial Home, a CCF orphanage located on the college campus.

Because of the great strides made by CCF in Japan under

his able direction, Seiji Giga was appointed by the Ministry of Welfare as Vice President of the Japanese Delegation to the Tenth International Conference of Social Work at Rome, Italy, in early 1961. Mr. Giga now is increasingly recognized as one of the leading authorities on child care in Japan.

Thus, while homes were being confiscated in mainland China and others were being formed in Korea, steady progress marked a pioneer path on the islands of Honshu, Hokkaido and Kyushu. As Dr. Clarke and CCF turned to Korea, much that was being learned in Japan would be applied in that besieged nation.

SIX

Though China Fall

Toward the end of 1946, the situation again began to worsen in China. After a brief respite, following the bloodbath of the Japanese War, a division took place within the Chinese armies. Throughout the latter months of 1945 and all of 1946, the United States attempted to restore the entente between Nationalists and Communists. During the last three years of World War II the rift between the two Chinese camps had been widening. Finally, in early 1947, General George C. Marshall, after prolonged effort, returned wearily to Washington. He was sharply critical of both and said that China's only hope lay in a coalition of liberals and conservatives under Chiang Kai-shek's leadership. After this diplomatic failure, civil war was inevitable.

Once again, millions of forlorn refugees took to the weary road. Once more the ones who suffered most were the children. The story of the conflict was told in microcosm by the case histories that began to flood the CCF office in Richmond:

"Chun-Kuei," reads one, "is a thoughtful little girl. Her father struggled through the many tragedies during World War II only to die of starvation in 1946. We do not know what became of her mother. Neighbors helped the child as much as they could. But when they had to flee before the Red

53

Armies, there was nothing more they could do for her. She was half-starved when UNRRA workers brought her to the CCF orphanage."

"Kuei-Lu," reads another case history, "was separated from his parents during one of the great mass flights from the marauding armies. He has never heard from them since. He has had to find food and shelter wherever he could, sometimes living in refugee camps until they were disbanded. More often he just lived on the streets, the highways or in the ditches. UNRRA workers eventually rescued him and brought him to the China's Children Fund orphanage."

Many of the children were transferred from one orphanage to another as the "People's Army" swept southward; yet many such children kept a perspective that was surprisingly mature. One, after such a mass transfer, wrote his "American mother":

Dear Sponsor:

I am very glad to receive your letter date the 18 November and contents have been fully note. Though we are far away from each other, I feel we meet each other when your letter come.

I always think of you because you are loving me. How can I repay you? I must pray that God will help me do.

In April this year our Home moved again. This time from Ping Shan to Fanling—on this side of the railway station. Around our Home there are some villages with farm lands. Our Home's opposite side in a hill with many trees on it. About half a mile in distance our home there is a little stream. During the summer maybe we can go there to swim. Its water is clean like a mirror, that the number of swimming fishes can be counted.

Over 60 of our Home-mates have been baptized. I am one of them. I am very happy to be a Christian.

Your supporting me is the special kindness of God. I am living happily in the Home. To receive your letter makes me happier. Thank you dear mother.

Your loving son,
Lee Ting Sun.

There were hundreds of others, however, who were not so happy as Ting Sun. Crushed by hunger, persecution and despair they were again dying without relief. Inflation, economic depression, lack of crucial materials, breakdown of rail and truck lines, and corruption in government finally brought about the collapse of the Nationalist regime on the China mainland. With the total loss of morale, thousands dropped their arms and fled while many others of the Nationalist troops defected to the enemy. The rest transferred to the islands of Hainan or Taiwan. On October 1, 1949, the Communist government formally declared Peking as its capital and entitled itself the People's Republic of China. Mao Tse-Tung was made the head of government with Chou En-Lai as prime minister.

Under these hammer blows, the CCF orphanages suffered continually heavier losses. In 1946 Dr. Clarke had made a flying trip to China where he had visited twenty-one of the orphanages and conferred with Dr. H. H. Kung who was Vice-Premier of the Nationalist Government. Despite the reassurances of that good man (for Dr. Kung was essentially a fine administrator) Dr. Clarke saw too many evidences of other things. He described these with a heavy heart:

"There was the rice line in Canton with its hungry men, women and children. Those at the end of the line had six hours of waiting, six hours of standing, sitting and edging forward in the hot tropical sun of Canton, for it took that long to reach the head of the line where the small portion of rice was being doled out. The authorities were afraid that if they started a second line the rice would not hold out.

"There was the old city across the creek from where I stayed in Shameen, the European section of Canton. There I saw children starving to death—mothers with youngsters in their arms who with their drawn, pinched faces looked more like mummies than human beings. Old women, terrible in their gaunt, shriveled hunger; old men whose beggar cups trembled in their hands like a candle flame in the wind. There was the whole population of Canton of over a million people with plague and cholera running rampant. There was always hunger."

The most distressing moments, however, came to Dr. Clarke as he sat in CCF's Canton office: "A steady stream of visitors came to see me. Pleas to expand here, to include more children in an orphanage there, tales of waiting lists, offers of buildings and missionary volunteer helpers, if only our organization would help. There was the same tense urgency in the voice of each who came!"

Desperation drove many hungry people in China. With the relentless advance of the Communist hordes the orphanages experienced some of the hardships of the previous war. The superintendents tried to carry on normal life as though nothing were happening. At first, the new Communist regime was fluid enough so that funds could be sent to the children. Many an American heart was wrung by the stories of suffering in the newspapers. A woman doctor wrote in haste to "adopt" a Chinese boy and upon receiving his picture was delighted. "I think you chose the right boy for me," she said. "I like his looks, and from my method of diagnosis, he seems to have the appearance and personal qualities for success and leadership. I have translated his name, Tak Tsai as 'Go-Getter.' The fact that of the thousands of children in the same condition the soldiers took him to the barracks speaks for a winning quality. I shall send him one of my mottoes, 'A winner never quits, and a quitter never wins!'

"I myself came up from the sidewalks of New York, through the free high school and college, later to earn my way through medical school—matriculating at the age of 35. I know what it means to fight one's way up from poverty, and if the time comes that he needs a little boost, I hope that I may be there to help him.

"Meanwhile, I am surprised at the thrill I had when I said to my mother and my friends, 'I have a son in China!' All the frustrated motherhood, suddenly released, did surprise even me—in spite of the hundreds of babies I have delivered. It was so different to say 'my son!' I recommend the experience for all the 'old maid' school teachers, editors, saleswomen, etc., that you can reach."

This letter was typical of the hundreds of Americans who wanted to say "my son in China" or "my daughter in China." And each was to know heartbreak as his or her "adopted" child was sealed off behind the "Bamboo Curtain."

The failing Nationalists saw only too clearly the importance of CCF and its American sponsors. In the spring of 1948, Madame T. V. Soong, sister-in-law of Madame Chiang Kai-shek and daughter of one of China's foremost families, visited the CCF Morning Star Orphanage in Canton. She was delighted with the administration of this model Home with its 500 children and its system of child-government. "In training our youngsters for democracy, we are insuring our future," she observed. To show her enthusiastic interest and support, she handed a generous check to Mr. Calvin Lee, the Home's superintendent, as she departed.

But many churches, alarmed by the Red incursions, withdrew their workers and funds long before CCF was willing to do so. In Chengtu, for example, 200 girls who had been receiving such care and support were suddenly cut off and were slowly starving to death. On the streets around that orphanage, there were hundreds more who were starving a bit more rapidly.

Verent Mills was sent by Dr. Clarke immediately to investigate. He found that it was "no fault of the matron that her youngsters were hungry. There were just not enough funds

to feed them properly." Although CCF already had two orphanages in Chengtu, Dr. Clarke could not turn his back on
these ravenous children. He turned to his many friends, who
gladly helped to assume the responsibilities of this girls' Home.

Mills, reporting again on the Chengtu situation, noted
the activities of one man in particular, who through his sacrifice and learning was responsible for much CCF success
in that city. "CCF is most fortunate," said he, "in having
such a man as Mr. T. C. Chue as superintendent of our Dewey
Orphanage." Dr. Dye of West China Union University had
hired Mr. Chue in 1919 as a coolie to watch his gate. It was
not long, however, before the doctor began to realize the po-
tential that was wrapped up in this young man who had
simply never been given an opportunity. Dr. Dye decided to
finance the boy through school. In a matter of only a few
years he went through primary school with flying colors; then
sent to Chungking for his high school education, he again
topped his class. He came home with a greater hunger for
knowledge than ever before. Finally the way opened for him
to enter Chengtu University.

Although it was customary in those days for a student to
receive a six-year course (three years in university, a year of
practical work, and a final two years back in university), Mr.
Chue lapped up his lessons like a hungry kitten in half that
time. Yet despite this brilliance he never lost his essential
humility. He determined to dedicate his life as a Christian
educator for boys and girls who like himself had had no opportunity for schooling. As soon as he had finished at the
university he started a school with fifty students. In the spring
of 1948, the enrollment numbered 1,668. Because of his own
background he made a special effort to educate the children
of coolies. And because of the traditional handicap of girls
in China, he provided training for young lasses who never,

for thousands of years back, had had female ancestors attending a school.

When the Communists finally reached Chengtu, Mr. Chue had the opportunity to flee with some missionary friends. He preferred, however, to stay with his children. Word came a year later through reliable sources that Mr. Chue had been liquidated by the People's Republic—a martyr to the cause of freedom.

This situation was the experience of many of the superintendents of CCF Homes. Refusing to abandon their young charges, they bravely stayed on, realizing more clearly day by day that their fate would be imprisonment and death.

As CCF's area of operation shrank, Dr. Clarke began to ask the inevitable question, "How long can we continue to send funds into Red China?" It was not an easy question to answer. The lives of thousands of little children were involved. The very existence of hundreds of staff workers whom he knew personally and loved greatly was at stake. "Are Americans to turn their backs completely on the people of China? Are we to say to the children of China, 'Of course, you had nothing to do with politics or Communism but, because of them, we are going to desert you. We are going to let you starve and die'?"

In 1949, Dr. Clarke again went to China to see what he could do for these helpless youngsters. Most of the mainland had been enveloped by the Communist Curtain. He was, however, able to get into South China, and there he wrote a letter of appeal, begging for sponsors' help: "Poor China!" he said, "I am writing this in Shanghai with the Communists getting closer and closer and no one knowing when the city will fall. We are under martial law and barbed-wire blockades are in many of the streets. The people seemed resigned, fearful of the Communists, dreading the approaching troops, but helpless. The streets are jammed with thousands of refugees, beg-

ging and pilfering and sleeping in alleyways or in the mud
beneath the city's bridges.

"We are using four kinds of currency, G.Y., American,
Hong Kong and the silver dollar. G.Y., of course, is the official
currency but, with a loaf of bread costing $80,000, of what
use is it? One spends hours trying to purchase the necessities—
that is, we Americans who have the money. I saw a dead baby
lying on the sidewalk this morning. I suppose its mother
hadn't the money for anything.

"I shall leave behind me our missionaries and their families
and the thousands of children in our orphanages who depend
on those homes for their very lives. And tens of thousands of
starving, dying children among the bewildered, exhausted refugees, fleeing before the advancing armies."

His heart was torn as he prepared to wing his way home-
ward again. "I don't want to think of them. Yet I can't escape
when my plane leaves tomorrow. I've seen the normal playing
and laughing of the children in our orphanages. I've talked
with them. They even got me to play shuttlecock with them.
I've held their little hands. Our workers are fathers and mothers to them, but I am the 'big father' from magic America.
It is my unhappy lot to try and get the money to keep them.

"It isn't just the children in our orphanages whom I am
leaving behind, either. It is the thousands of others who will
starve to death in the next month. Indeed, I asked Superintendent Dibden at our Fanling Orphanage, 'How many of
these would be alive today, if you had not taken them in?'
She turned to me in surprise; 'None,' she said without hesita-
tion. 'They would all have died!' "

In concluding his letter, he wrote thoughtfully, "The only
prayer I made in China that I can remember is the one I
made when I saw that dead baby on the sidewalk, 'By your
death, little baby, may others be saved.' "

At first, the Red government used a "velvet glove." Verent

Mills was sent by Dr. Clarke to inspect the Homes still remaining in Peiping in November of 1949. He reported the children all well and happy. There had been weeks in early 1949 when communications had been cut off. Then the lines were re-established and were kept open for the next eighteen months. The children, he said, had some "thrilling stories to tell." The Canaan Orphanage in Peiping, as well as the Hsiang Shan Home, had found themselves right on the front lines. Cannonading shook the walls, rifle fire cracked all around, and of course the children were terrified. But for the time being they were safe.

The tide was running fast now, however. By November of 1949, Dr. Clarke reported to one of CCF's sponsors, "Just recently the Communists captured Canton. The orphanage where your child is located is about 20 miles from that city. I am not sure whether the Communists have taken that particular section yet or not. Twenty miles means more in China than it does in America and there is a river to be crossed. That particular section where your child is located was the headquarters for guerillas in the Japanese War, so there may still be some left there, but we do have ways of keeping in touch with the orphanage.

"If you wish to send a birthday cash gift to your child, we shall be glad to send a credit slip to Hong Kong for you. Our superintendent in Canton goes over to Hong Kong, which is less than 100 miles away, once a week to get funds that are needed for our seven orphanages in and around Canton. He will be able to purchase things in Canton for your child and see that the youngster receives them."

By late 1950, the handwriting on the wall was all too clear. CCF had continued to send funds into mainland China as long as it safely could. Indeed, the United States State Department had given special permission to Dr. Clarke to send money even after the freezing of Chinese assets. Finally, the inevitable occurred.

・Reporting from Hong Kong in early 1951, Verent Mills told Dr. Clarke, "The city is jammed with refugees and the country roads are black with them. The Hong Kong Government is doing all that it can but the problem is a terrific one. In fleeing from Communism, the refugees left all their worldly goods behind them and they are destitute. There are so many orphan children among them—children whose parents died of hunger and exposure in their flight. Naturally, they are looking to CCF's chain of orphanages in order to help these bewildered, parentless and hungry children. Expansion of our work is urgent and imperative!"

Reluctantly, Dr. Clarke wrote to each of the thousands of sponsors who was helping a child in China that, "CCF will make every effort to continue to help your child. However, should change of circumstances involve any danger of funds falling into the wrong hands, or otherwise make our work inoperable on the China mainland, we want you to know that we shall then transfer all our commitments to non-Communist areas where we are being desperately urged to increase our already established orphanages. In some cases we may be able to move more of our children—small numbers at a time— to places of greater security."

"At any rate," he continued, "please be assured that we shall keep you informed in event of any change in your "adoption." For your part, at this critical time when Communism and Democracy are in desperate conflict, may we urge that you continue your interest and your help and your prayers so that there may be as little suffering as possible among the children we have loved, cared for, and converted to our Christian faith."

And continue their interest they did, by the thousands— these kindly friends of CCF! With the transfer of hundreds of children to safe areas in Hong Kong under the British flag, the sponsors helped with enthusiasm. But they waited also with bated breath for those final words of regret from Dr. Clarke. The words came two months later: "The orphanages are no longer permitted to accept funds from us. It is not that the Red government will provide for the children now. It is simply that no friendly relationship with America will be permitted by the Red overlords!"

For the orphanage children who were so far inland they could not be transferred to Hong Kong, Macao or Taiwan, there was suffering and death. Reports soon leaked out of Red China that these youngsters had been ousted from the CCF Homes by soldiers of the "People's Republic." A heartbreaking letter from one such youngster, Kwang San Sun, was smuggled to Dr. Clarke a few months later: "A soldier gave me a small bag of rice and told me to leave. I asked him, 'But where shall I go?' He snapped at me gruffly, 'Wherever you want!'" The saddest and most poignant part of the letter, however, was the closing, where the child said, "Please, dear Dr. Clarke, remember that I will never forget your kindness. Tell my dear sponsor also that I will never forget his goodness to me, no matter what happens!"

The children were not the only ones to suffer. Chinese staff workers and superintendents were often interned. Some were imprisoned and others were even executed for collaborating with the Americans. Reverend Verent Mills was put under house arrest in his Shanghai home. For six long months during those trying times in 1949, he was required to rise at 5:00 A.M. and report to the Police Headquarters. Through the tedious hours he waited for questioning, only to be told to "come back tomorrow." Finally, he was accused by the government officials of spying. He protested his innocence, of course, but to no avail. "Aren't you the Mills who issued this statement from Canton last year?" they would ask. They then read some unfamiliar passages from a document. He denied any knowledge of the matter and was ordered to return, again and again. He says that, "It was only after endless effort on the part of Mr. Chang An Teh, CCF's Secretary for the North China District, with other friends who put their lives in jeopardy as unconditional guarantors that we were set free. Eventually (it seemed like a miracle) the Communists released us and we were permitted to travel to Hong Kong and freedom."

Others were not so fortunate. The families of missionaries who had not escaped in time were held as hostages. Some straggled across the famous Lowu Escape Bridge years later, thin and faded, hollow shadows of former selves. Many disappeared, never to be heard from again—swallowed in the maw of a vengeful regime.

The final word on the unfortunate situation came from Dr. Clarke who wrote with a grieving heart to one of the sponsors: "I am afraid I have bad news for you. Up until the first of this year (1951) we were able to get funds in perfect safety to Leung Maan Shing, your child, but since that time the Communists have been putting on a 'hate campaign' against America. This does not mean that the average Chinese hates America. I believe 90 per cent of the Chinese look upon America as China's best friend. But it is almost impossible to conceive of the evil and cruelty of the gangster Communist leaders who are killing thousands of their countrymen and starving thousands more. It is an extremely tragic situation with blood flowing like water . . ."

The flood of letters previously flowing to the children and orphanages halted abruptly. "We do not dare even to write to these superintendents," he explained, "because if it was learned by the Communists that they received letters from Americans, it would result in punishment and perhaps even death."

In commenting on his internment and experience with the Communists, Verent Mills stated, "At first I thought, along with many missionaries, that they were instituting some beneficial 'agrarian reform' for China. But after I had these six months of grueling interrogation and saw with my own eyes the atrocities performed by them, I quickly changed my mind. I am now convinced that no compromise is possible with Marxist Communism in any form!"

Regretfully, CCF said goodbye to the 5,113 children of the 46 orphanages in China. A conservative estimate of the property values lost to Communist "appropriation" by CCF ranges between one and two million dollars.

There was little time to look backward, however. CCF tried to transfer as many of its children as possible down the Pearl River to Hong Kong. Dr. Clarke immediately authorized the establishment of a Welfare Center at Rennie's Mills in Kowloon. Into this small area thousands of desperate folk poured in 1951. Soup kitchens, rice dispensaries, milk depots were erected. Little children in rags were gathered and placed in hastily formed Homes.

At the same time, CCF turned its eyes toward the hungry children in Macao and Taiwan. In May of 1951, Dr. Clarke was writing, "We still have fifteen Chinese orphanages in non-Communist territory in places like Malaya, Formosa and Hong Kong. In Hong Kong," he re-emphasized, "the needs are particularly great because it is just across the border from Red China and is filled with refugees who were obliged to leave all their worldly possessions behind them and arrived in Hong Kong destitute. In addition to this," he reminded his many friends, "we have orphanages in ten other countries. . . For instance, because of the refugee problem in Korea we have increased the number of orphanages from five to thirteen."

The great majority of sponsors stood loyally by CCF during

these drastic changes. One of them, an eminent scholar and professor at Princeton said, "It is a pity to think of the miserable plight of so many children in those parts of the world. I am afraid that sometimes the West is to be blamed directly or indirectly for much of that suffering. As you may imagine, I feel very sorry for my little Chinese girl, and I can only hope and pray that with the foundation laid in the orphanage she will be able to grow up into a fine, upright, Christian woman. . . The wonderful work which you and your Committee are carrying on is one of the finest demonstrations of the power of Christ in this modern world of hatred!"

It has been a constant source of amazement to Dr. Clarke to find that, despite the vindictiveness of Red China toward Christianity, there are churchmen who feel that Communism has been "good" for China. In 1950, Protestant mission sources estimated that there were 900,000 Chinese Protestants and about 2,000 missionaries. In addition, there were, according to both church and unofficial reports, about 3,000,000 Roman Catholic Chinese with 5,500 foreign missionaries. As soon as the Chinese Communists came to power they declared all-out war on foreign missions. They charged that these missionaries were the "cultural wing of Western Imperialism."

This all-out effort gathered momentum after Red China entered the Korean War. It became a part of the general "hate-America" drive and culminated in the increasing number of arrests of missionaries, of whom Verent Mills was one out of hundreds. By the middle of 1951 the "official" deaths of three missionaries in prison were acknowledged by the Reds—Dr. William L. Wallace, Warren L. Winter, both of whom were Protestants, and Bishop Francis X. Ford, a Roman Catholic. The unofficial count will never be known.

Beginning in 1950, these "un-ugly Americans" who had dedicated their lives, fortunes and love to the help and healing of the Chinese began to pour across the Lowu Bridge on the

Hong Kong-Kwangtung frontier. They came by the thousands. An eye-witness to this distressing sight reported, "I saw every kind. Some looked all right. Others couldn't walk or stand after the torture (in prison) of segregation, starvation, having their hands tied behind their backs—and most important— questioning, questioning, questioning, day and night."

According to a *New York Times* dispatch of May 14, 1956, "The Communists have virtually completed the liquidation of a century-and-a-half and more of foreign missionary work in China." Confiscated were the hundreds of schools, colleges, hospitals, orphanages, libraries and countless other Christian institutions that long had benefited China. Gone, too, were the millions that had been spent annually on healing, school- ing, preaching and counseling. But most seriously, gone was the spirit of Christ that had been the hope of the future of China.

SEVEN

Calamity In the Land
of Morning Calm

In early 1949, sporadic Communist revolts began to break out in South Korea. An uneasy truce had existed along the 38th Parallel for almost four years, due to the unsettled Korean unification problem. In the North, a Russian-inspired government had been training and equipping an army, 100,000 strong. In the South, a government conceived in democratic methods struggled under Syngman Rhee's leadership to keep stride and to build a handicapped economy.

In January and February of 1949, 12,000 "insurgents" in Yosu, South Korea, broke into open revolt. Rhee's ROK Army quickly quelled this rebellion, only to be faced with a similar military "grass-fire" on Cheju Island, off Korea's southern coast. Here, 15,000 more Communist-inspired rebels rose up to force a coup. This, too, was rapidly squelched by Rhee's regulars.

South Korea, however, was made increasingly uneasy by well-founded rumors that North Koreans were massing troops along the 38th Parallel and that invasion was imminent. Throughout the unhappy land, there were continual evidences of lawlessness. On March 17, Mrs. Horace H. Underwood,

CCF's committee chairman for Korea, was assassinated by a Communist guerilla. This distinguished missionary, a member of the famous Underwood Typewriter family that helped to initiate Christian missions in Korea, was savagely murdered while protecting one of her staff members. Mrs. Underwood had just completed a monumental task of organizing "The Seoul Home for Girls" when the treacherous blow fell. Dr. Horace Underwood, her husband, wrote to Dr. Clarke shortly after her death. "Mrs. Underwood spent the last month of her life working almost frantically to get the legal foundations of the 'Home for Girls in Need' set up. All arrangements were completed and she told me the morning she died, 'Tomorrow I go to the court to sign the last papers.' "

She was never able to sign the papers, but others, signing in her stead, changed the name of the orphanage to the Ethel Underwood Home in her memory. Commencing in 1945, with the flight of men, women and children from North Korean tyranny, the refugee problem had become acute. It was estimated with considerable accuracy that 6,000,000 of these helpless folk had crowded across the 38th Parallel during the period between 1945 and 1949. Ethel Underwood's heart went out to these people, "But," said she, "the little girls from ten years to sixteen are the most pitiable. They are the ones most subjected to abuse, cold, hunger and every moral danger." Looking back over Korea's history, she recalled, "Many years ago, girls in Korea were sent from home at an early age to learn to be good daughters-in-law. This was followed by a period when the girls became apprentices in factories. inns and home industries." After V-J Day, "Every Korean home still had a little servant girl. Most have been treated well, are encouraged to keep in touch with their families and eventually marry into suitable homes," she continued. "But often in these terrible days there just is no family. The 'master' sends the girl out to work, or sends her into the street to work, to beg, to sell all

types of things and even to deal in stolen goods. Often they are
arrested, but when no one makes a charge, they are 'washed
up,' given food, kept for the legal three days and then sent
back on the streets again. Their home is the coldest corner,
their food is the scrapings from the family bowls, their clothes
are rags, their earnings belong to their masters. These poor
girls are unprotected from every brutality, greed or passion of
any evil person!"

This, then, was the vision and compassion of Ethel Underwood and for it she willingly gave her life. The needs were overwhelming in the Seoul of 1949 with 1,700,000 people and half
of them refugees. This, too, was the vision and compassion of
Calvitt Clarke, which had caused him to establish a Korean
Committee in 1948, and to increase CCF's aid to more and
more orphanages each month.

In the moments of sorrow at the loss of such a staunch
friend of children and of such a friend of the work of CCF,
Dr. Clarke wrote these words: "Ethel Underwood, China's
Children Fund Chairman in Korea, was assassinated by Communists on March 17th. Because of its deep forgiving Christian spirit and its tribute to a noble woman, we reproduce a
letter just received from Dr. Horace H. Underwood, Presbyterian missionary, CCF Treasurer and bereaved husband."
Thereafter followed this letter which did, indeed, show forth
the spirit of Christ:

Your friend and my dear wife has gone to be with God.
There is no one of whom it is so impossible to believe that
death is the grave as of a Christian spirit like hers.

In a sense her going was blessed. She taught her class of boys
whom she loved, she came back to a meeting in her home of
women whom she loved. Two armed men broke in. She
grappled with one and the other shot her. She died in a short
time apparently without great pain—no lingering illness.

She taught her class at 1:00 P.M. and came home at Two

O'Clock for a meeting of the faculty women's club. The meeting was in progress when a man came through the back door and kitchen and another came in the front door. She saw the man struggling with the cook and ran out. She apparently grappled with the man who came through the front door, and the man who came through the back door knocked down the cook and fired twice. One shot entered her back and passed out under her right breast.

After the man fled, the others tried to make her comfortable on the floor, and she said in Korean, "It is all right." She did not speak again. They got a mattress and a car and rushed her to the hospital and called us (Horace, Joan, John and I). We rushed to the hospital but she was gone when I got there, and apparently died on the way there.

The Communists have recently been threatening to kill those who are "teaching capitalism." They have also been recently attacking women and children as the best way to terrify the men. I have long said that some day the Communists would decide that the time had come to kill some well-known American "to show the world that the Koreans hate the American imperialists." It is no exaggeration to say that there was probably no one so widely loved in all Korea as Mrs. Underwood and this made her a good mark. She would feel most deeply hurt (could she still be further hurt) if through her the good name of Korea was tarnished. I beg of you in her name not to feel that Koreans are to blame. Already (within two hours of the affair) we have heard from the President of Korea, the Prime Minister, a representative of the Assembly and other high officials. They are doing everything in their power to catch the assassins, though neither Ethel nor I want any Korean executed on our account.

I cannot do her work, I cannot write her letters. You will find me a poor correspondent. She knew and loved you all. She knew where you lived, what happened to you, and rejoiced with or sympathized with you in your joys and sorrows. I will try to do so. Korea still needs your relief packages. I will try to acknowledge them.

We shall go on as best we can—God will give me strength I believe. I am writing this in the wee hours of the morning, just twelve hours after she was killed. I am going to get Joan to mimeograph it and address the twelve hundred or fifteen hun-

dred envelopes that are needed to reach you. I do not know
when this will be done.

She loved you, and she loved to think that you loved and
thought of Korea. She would have you continue that thought,
that love, those prayers. We all need prayers; our children, I,
the Koreans, the Communists. "Prayer availeth much."

> Let us have those prayers for
> Korea. Yours in the grief of
> loss and in the joy of Faith
> Horace Underwood

By the summer of 1949, CCF was helping children in five
orphanages. They were drawn from the thousands of refugees
and apparently had lost their parents long since. They were
found sleeping in the streets or in the ditches along the country
roads. Many had resorted to begging or stealing. Many were
emaciated with hunger and neglect. These first five Homes in
Korea were the Salvation Army Boys' Home, the Salvation
Army Girls' Home, the Seoul Girls' Home (the one founded
by Mrs. Underwood), the Seoul Children's Home at An
Yang (founded by Dr. Oh) and the Chongju Home (founded
by Mrs. Harry Hill).

The youngsters in each of these Homes were fed, clothed,
educated and loved in a way that they could never have hoped
for before. The Homes also conducted classes in vocational
training such as tailoring, shoemaking, carpentry, agriculture
and weaving. They were a Godsend to a disheartened nation.
But even this important help was soon to be terribly hampered
by the forces of evil.

On June 25, 1950, the dam broke and the flood waters of
Communism spilled over the 38th Parallel. By June 27, the
North Korean troops marched through the streets of Seoul.
Panic seized President Rhee's ROK Army, and they fled in
utter rout before the well-trained and well-equipped forces
from the North. There is little doubt, according to the experts,

that they would have been swept to Pusan at the nation's southern extremity had not President Truman ordered American troops into action. These soldiers, mainly green and unseasoned boys who had been part of the peacetime Occupation Forces in Japan, gave a wonderful account of themselves. Under-equipped and under-trained, they fought a delaying action until help could arrive. The invasion tide was halted at Taejon by these men.

After much jockeying and negotiation in the United Nations General Assembly, General Douglas MacArthur was appointed Commander-in-Chief of the U.N. Emergency Force. Bloody hand-to-hand fighting was waged in and around Taejon until the brilliant Inchon Landing on September 15. In this movement, the U.N. Forces penetrated the vulnerable right flank of the enemy. Now it was the turn of the Communists to retreat in terror. On September 29 the South Korean troops, now allied with the U.N. Forces re-entered Seoul. In early October they crossed the 38th Parallel and on October 19th they marched triumphantly into the North Korean capital of Pyongyang. As they neared the Yalu River at the northern border, however, a new source of trouble presented itself.

On November 5th the first troops of "volunteers" from Red China poured over the border from Manchuria and drove the U.N. Forces back in a staggering blow. Icy blasts from the barren mountains also brought great suffering to soldier and civilian alike. By Christmas Day, Seoul was being evacuated for the second time. Pathetic refugees streamed out of the city carrying all their worldly possessions in oxcarts and bearing children on their backs.

Flushed with success, the Communists resorted to every ruse that evil minds could invent. When these refugee columns neared the U.N. lines, the Allied soldiers allowed them to go through. Quickly detecting this humanitarianism as a "weakness," great numbers of the Red guerillas joined the refugee lines. When U.N. soldiers discovered this, greater security measures were exercised to prevent infiltration. The Communists then countered with a new ruse. It was discovered that a Red soldier had slaughtered a mother, disrobed her, donned her clothing, grasped her children by the hand and led them toward the U.N. lines. This was repeated a thousand fold. In other instances, Communist women were disguised as refugees. Under their clothing the Reds hid dynamite and ammunition. One woman was searched and found to have yards of primer cord for fuses wrapped around her waist.

When such things began to happen with increasing frequency, the Allied lines were closed to refugees. This threw the hapless creatures back toward the Communist emplacements. The Reds, in turn, trained rifle fire on them as human targets. Thus caught in a "no man's land" trap, many refugees gave up in despair and threw themselves into the line of fire purposely. Others, leaning against the bitter winds and bowed under their pitiful belongings, waited hopelessly for the end.

As the Communists approached one of CCF's orphanages after another, the superintendents were forced to evacuate the youngsters and lead them to safety farther south. Unable to carry much food, they were soon on the verge of starvation. Here again was evidence of the Christian love and concern shown by American G.I.'s. Many of them took helpless tots into their arms and fed them from K-rations, or with stale bread and powdered milk.

The stories told by these youngsters were heartbreaking. "My mother was shot and killed. I have no home," said one. "A crowd of people separated me from Daddy and Mother. I never saw them again," said another. The G.I.'s picked them up along the frozen roads or found them "sleeping" their final sleep in an icy ditch. There was no place to go, no place to hide, and they perished by the thousands.

Brutality was added to brutality by the Communists as the

time passed. *The National Geographic* in one article told how North Korean troops had stoned groups of little beggar lads. A tiny boy was slashed to death because he had a morsel of G.I. boot polish in his shoeshine kit. Others thought to be friendly with Americans were found with ripped arms and legs, or with eyes pierced by sticks. Soldier and civilian alike were subjected to unmentionable tortures.

As they were driven southward their feet became sore from the frozen earth and snow. River after river edged with jagged ice had to be forded. Most of the bridges, splintered by repeated bombings, were nothing but bare girders, if that. Some desperate folk, more agile than the others, clambered over the girders. Some of these slipped into the river halfway across. Those too over-burdened to try this "tight-rope" feat had to plunge into the icy waters. At one such crossing, women, holding babies aloft over their heads slid down the north bank into the chill stream. Many of them lost their footing in mid-current and their infants were swept away from them to certain death. Only half of those who ventured in on the north bank finally made it to the southern edge. Often a whole family would be drowned together. Most smaller children died in attempting to ford. No one knows the number of casualties who thus perished. But with the Communists on their heels, the lines of refugees, mile after mile of them, kept plunging in and trying—and dying.

By January 15, 1951, the Red Army had reached Suwan and Kangnung. The pounding guns and bombs kept the hapless refugees moving. One eye-witness said, "In contrast to the early panic of the war's opening days, the moving streams of people now showed characteristic Oriental fatalism. A 'kind of order' had developed as these millions of homeless folk eddied southward to Pusan. Finally, with nowhere else to go they became 'wards of the U.N. Forces.' "

During this time, planes had dropped 42,000 tons of bombs

on Korea—more than all the bombs dropped on Germany for the year 1942, according to General O'Donnell's report to the President from Tokyo.

With such constant pressure, the tide of battle again changed. The Communist invaders were thrown back. On March 15th the U.N. armies entered Seoul for the second time. On March 31st they recrossed the 38th Parallel and were making a fair bid to reach the Yalu River once more. This seemed to be a strategic moment for both sides to sue for a cease-fire. There was to be a long-drawn-out period of proposal and counter-proposal at Panmunjom before the final Armistice was signed on July 27, 1953. But it provided a breathing spell when CCF with hundreds of others would help to bind up the wounds.

During the last retreat toward Pusan, an Air Force colonel earned well-deserved acclaim for the transfer of homeless CCF youngsters to a safe retreat on Cheju Island. This famous person was Dean Hess of the Fifth Air Force. On December 7, 1941, he had been a Protestant pastor in a church located in Marietta, Ohio. On that Sunday he made a tremendous decision. "I could not," he said, "ask my parishioners to sacrifice themselves and their sons, unless I, too, was willing to do so." With this decision taken, he became a fighter pilot for the United States Air Force. During World War II and the Korean War he flew over 300 combat missions. He was decorated on many occasions for his courage and daring.

During the Korean War he was largely responsible for the training of raw recruits into a South Korean Air Force. He succeeded so well that Syngman Rhee tendered him Korea's highest military award.

Most Americans, however, remember him for the role he played in initiating "Operation Kiddie-Car." As the Communist forces rolled toward Seoul in December of 1950, thousands of homeless children gathered around the army camps.

Hess' heart was deeply moved by these tots. Guiding them to the airport in Seoul, he appealed to his Commander for help. As the Communists were all but knocking on the city gates, a contingent of planes flew in to pick up these waifs and transport them to Cheju Island off the southern tip of Korea. The "mother" who accompanied this big family of helpless children was Mrs. On Soon Whang, one of Korea's outstanding social welfare leaders, who was appointed to this task by President Syngman Rhee. Later, with the help of CCF, they were able to establish the Orphans' Home of Korea. G.I.'s stationed on the island cheerfully lent their muscle to repairing the old Agricultural School so that the children might be sheltered. At the same time, Dr. Clarke sent out appeals to hundreds of American friends to "adopt" these needy little ones. The response was overwhelming.

This dramatic tale so captured America's heart that it was eventually made into a motion picture entitled "Battle Hymn," with the starring actor Don Defore. An interesting sequel to the story involves Defore's own family. When he traveled to Korea for on-location shots, he took his fourteen-year-old daughter Penny. There she saw the filming of the story and met some of the children whose lives had been saved through the efforts of Hess and CCF. So impressed was she that she determined to dedicate her life to working with children. Don Defore and his wife promised she could, "when you're 18"—saying to themselves for four years, "Penny will outgrow this fantastic idea." But in December of 1960 she packed her things to go to the Orphans' Home of Korea. During those four years, between her fourteenth and eighteenth birthdays, she had donated $750.00 from money made by modeling, personal appearances and selling cookies at the University High School in Los Angeles. During that period she had also written many times to Colonel Hess telling of her plans and her desire to become a missionary.

Penny's parents have been a bit nonplussed by the whole thing. "We all tried to talk her out of it," Defore admitted. "But when a determined girl like Penny decides she must do something which she feels very, very deeply is right, how can we convince her otherwise? How can you tell her she's doing wrong? So, after four years, we've given in and are happy for her—because we know she feels seriously and deeply about this." Here is another example of the serious-minded young people who can be numbered with the thousands of "un-ugly Americans."

One of the factors in Penny's resolution may have been the Cheju cemetery—two hundred small mounds with no markers or stones. These are the resting places of those children without parents or homes who died without even an identity. Colonel Hess dreamed of the day when he could consecrate a simple stone to these youngsters with the words, "Dedicated to the Memory of Those Whom We Could Not Save." He recalled one of these three-year-old mites who died in his arms. The child had suffered so from malnutrition that he was only the size of a newborn infant. His resistance was so low that he succumbed to whooping cough. "When he coughed his last, a look of peace finally came over his face . . . I knew that Christ had opened heaven's door and let him in."

When the dust and smoke of the battle had settled, the losses were found to be heavy. The casualties for the United States alone were 144,173, of which 25,604 were dead. The heaviest loser, of course, was South Korea whose casualty list accounted for 1,312,836 with 415,004 of them dead or missing. No accounting was ever forthcoming from North Korea or from Red China although their losses must have been disastrous.

In addition to all this bloodshed, the war had caused monstrous damage to the economy and living conditions of Korea. Several million civilians had died, either violently or by starvation. Ten million were homeless in South Korea alone. By 1955 the United States had given $1,500,000,000 for reconstruction and yet this barely scratched the surface so great was the need.

By mid-1951 Christian Children's Fund had increased its number of orphanages in Korea from five to seventeen. Dr. Clarke was well aware, however, that this was but a drop in the ocean. He kept his staff workers on the go every instant.

Cases like that of Ell Im, a twelve-year-old little girl who died in the snow on a Seoul street were all too common. His heart was heavy as he reconstructed her sad story for CCF's sponsors: "Ell Im tried to huddle closer in the corner of the doorway," he wrote, "but still the whirling snow reached her. She pulled at her dress to keep the snow from her neck and shoulders. The worn, thin cloth tore and exposed her still more to the icy needles stabbing at her flesh. She whimpered in misery. It was still early in the night. How could she stand it hour after hour through the long darkness? She wondered dejectedly whether the morning would be any better? Even without the snow, the day before she had found nothing to eat—not one bite. She thought back to those days before she and her mother searched in the prison yard for her father's body. They had been told he had been executed because he was a preacher. There were so many bodies and, trembling, Ell Im helped her mother turn some of them over so they could be sure not to miss her father. She kept hoping they would not find him, that he was not there. But they did find him.

"A week later, when Ell Im woke in the morning, her mother was gone. She waited a lonely week and then gave up; her mother would have returned if she could have. Then Ell Im joined the other refugees. Before all these things happened, there had been food and warmth and happiness. The tears froze on Ell Im's cheeks. The wind was stronger now, the snow fell faster, but she no longer trembled and tried to hunch herself tighter, fighting the cold. She relaxed and was drowsy.

"Early the next morning two G.I.'s came down the street. 'Look,' one pointed, 'that kid is a goner.' He bent over and brushed the snow away. 'Why, it's a girl, a little girl about twelve, I guess.'

"The other soldier shook his head. 'She wasn't here when I passed about seven last night. I wish the poor little thing had been. I bet, even if they are overcrowded, I could have persuaded that Christian Children's Fund orphanage to take her in.'

" 'Maybe you could have. But it's too late now. Nothing we can do. She's been dead for hours. You can see that. I never thought I would see things like this in Korea. Fighting—yes. But not little starved kids, dead and half-buried in the snow.' "

There were between 50,000 and 100,000 of these youngsters who had been orphaned. They ran the streets. They died in the gutters. They scrambled for food. They resorted to stealing and violence. The older girls sold their bodies for a scrap of food.

Verent Mills was continuously on the go, searching for facilities to house these youngsters, writing desperately to Dr. Clarke for additional funds to feed them. He described some of the experience that he had seen scores of times:

"Traveling by train, I noticed that at every station these starving waifs swarmed aboard and would look under the seats, going through anything they could find on the floor, hoping to see something to eat. While the train was stopped at Taejon, I was eating my lunch of cold boiled rice with beans, a small piece of fried fish and some Kimchi (Korean pickle, made of cabbage, onions, garlic and red peppers). Beside this, there was a small portion of shredded, dried octopus. The train had no sooner came to a halt when these dirty, hungry, pitiful little fellows came pushing their way through the crowded coach.

The police could not stop them. One little boy squeezed over by me. I observed the longing look in his eyes and turned over what was left of my lunch to him. He scooped it up with his hand and stuffed it into his mouth desperately. Had he waited another minute, or been a little slow, some of the other children would have snatched it from him."

Traveling to the southwestern corner of Korea, Mills came to one of the larger cities. "In the station at Mokpo," he related, "I walked down the platform to keep warm. Near the far end I heard crying and found a forsaken little fellow squatted in the corner. He held an old G.I. fatigue shirt over his head and shuddered, trying to keep warm. His face was filthy dirty, while his whole tiny body quivered with the cold. I gave him some money and told him to buy food, but he was too weak to get up.

"Sights like this," said Mills, "were to be seen everywhere. The children's heads were covered with scurvy, ringworm, and other scabs. Their hair was matted into little tufts by the hardened pus from their sores. Their stomachs were swollen, while their necks, legs and arms were like sticks. The dry skin of their bodies, hung over them like loose bags."

This, then, was the situation that CCF faced in late 1951. Telling the story to Americans, Dr. Clarke found their response the most generous he had ever known. Binding up the wounds of Korea was made possible by thousands of Americans who gladly shared.

EIGHT

And Bind Up the Children's Wounds

KWANGJU was one of the first places to receive the attention of CCF's staff. War had entered and re-entered this city in the heart of South Korea. The armies had swept back and forth and the people had bled and died.

Some Korean Methodists began picking up babies as they were abandoned and orphaned. They were tiny wizened things, with hardly a chance for survival. Some of them were pale, wan, undernourished infants, wrapped carefully and left hopefully in public places—the station . . . the store . . . the doorstep. Some babies were found in rags or paper wrappings. Some were bundled in their mothers' last warm garments— lost in the big and terrified refugee movements.

These church folk found a two storey brick building on the outskirts of town. It was relatively undamaged by shelling. And Choong Hyun proved to be the first Babies' Home in the whole Province. In the beginning whole milk and rice often could not be found. On those lean days, milk had to be stretched with water, and the rice had to be made into a thin broth. During the first year there were times when CCF

82

and the Methodist staff thought their doors would have to be closed.

Somehow, the Home came through. Life moved along quite simply, for the orphanage had the basic essentials—dedicated love and concern. It was able to add another busy kitchen— a play room—a dining room. Its rooms became lined with immaculate cribs and beds that had been donated by American Christians.

One such American Christian was Bob Hull, an American soldier, later to become feature writer for *The East Ohio News*. He told the story of the way he found one tot—a little girl who was later brought to CCF's Choong Hyun Orphanage: "Mi Mi Choi wouldn't smile. But that was before she had a name. A name makes a difference. Now she grins. Sometimes she can even manage a laugh.

"They found her when she was only three, in a doorway, on the day that war came to Seoul. When I appeared at Choong Hyun Orphanage a year later, Mi Mi was called from her cottage and lined up with seven close-cropped boys according to size. She was the short end.

"With me was a young social worker. Together we scanned the children studying each face. The social worker told me of a plan whereby orphan youngsters could be 'adopted' on a sponsorship basis. The cost was a specified monthly donation used for the children's food and expense.

" 'There must be a gimmick,' I had insisted. 'Somebody has a racket.'

"The worker brought me to the Choong Hyun Home to see for myself.

" 'Take your pick,' she said.

" 'I guess I'll take the girl,' I said, 'the little glum one.'

"And then came the problem of naming her. I was in a fix.

" 'What name will suit her? I asked several Korean teachers who were standing by.

" 'Mi Mi,' someone suggested. 'It means "beautiful" in Korean.' I liked the sound of it in both languages.

"Months later when I left for the States and military separation, I was still very much Mi Mi's 'Papa-san.' I sent her boxes of clothes and toys at Christmas time, and she sent back picture valentines and letters written by a nurse who acted as 'secretary.'

"I will always remember her, as my little girl with a hole in her mitten, waving to my jeep in the distance."

It was in this Home, too, that CCF cooperated with the Methodist Church by supplying a building for another of Korea's urgent needs. This structure was devoted to the sheltering of children of mixed-blood parentage.

As in other war-torn countries, the moral fibre frayed as a result of the desperate hunger. By 1956, it was estimated that there were between 200,000 and 400,000 prostitutes in Korea. In the South Korean capital, 10,000 of these formed themselves into a body called the Seoul Prostitutes' Union. They termed themselves "Yang-Ki-Bels," and were picked up—not singly but in truckloads—and transported to areas of "assignation."

Although Seoul and Pusan were the main centers for such immoral conditions, they were actually spread throughout the whole of Korea. Mokpo, Chongju, Taejon and Taegu found them by the thousands, as did hundreds of smaller towns. These women gathered around the army camps and depots, and alliances with the men of the U.N. Forces resulted in many illegitimate children. It was to orient these "fatherless" mixed-blood youngsters and others for adoption abroad that CCF's sponsors supplied the funds to build a special wing at Choong Hyun. From this Wing, hundreds of children both mixed-blood and Korean have been flown to adopting parents in the United States. Placed through such agencies as International Social Service (with headquarters in New York City) as well as Child Placement and others, these youngsters have become members of the American community.

Shortly after this orphanage was founded, a young Christian pastor was crossing the bridge at Taejon. He noticed a ragged, hungry-looking urchin leaning against the parapet. Asking the youngster about his family, the minister received the reply, "I have none. My mother was killed by a bomb. My father was shot by the North Koreans." Putting his arm around the boy's shoulder he took him home and began to care for the child from his meagre salary. Soon, Mr. Kim gathered more of these little fellows as they drifted through the streets of Taejon. His quarters were far too cramped to accommodate so many and he set up a small camp on the outskirts of town. So many hungry mouths quickly taxed Mr. Kim's resources, but other Christians were beginning to take an interest. An old Japanese house was donated to him as the cold winter of 1953 drew near. Then a CCF staff member discovered what he was doing. Soon Dr. Clarke had been notified and sponsors were found who were glad to "adopt" these children.

In looking around, however, Mr. Kim's heart was stirred. Taejon had been called the "Hiroshima of Korea" because the city was entirely flattened by the repeated bombings in 1950 and 1951. In this razed area, the survivors built their pathetic "haka-bans," or "packing-box houses." Fashioned of cardboard, bits of wood, flattened tin, tar paper and canvas, such houses are a familiar sight everywhere in Korea. But in Taejon, for several years they were the entire structural composition of the city. In the midst of this slum condition were hundreds of children who were homeless and hungry. With his vision of Christian care, he was soon fashioning what is known today as "Bethel Won"—Bethel Home.

Here today, on clean, warm "Ondol" floors—the world's first "radiant heated" floors were invented here in Korea;

they are covered with oiled linoleum-like paper—the tiny ones tumble about and are the special delight of their nurses. Here, too, are new sleeping quarters and a big dining room (at night it doubles as a study hall) with its polished pine floor. Surrounding the newly-constructed buildings are playgrounds and gardens. Mr. Kim's dream has come true. Each child is not only cared for but is being taught a trade. A boy may learn how to tailor, to carpenter, to cut hair or to weave. A girl, in addition to cooking and housekeeping, may learn how to knit, to sew, or to do hairdressing. Recreation time is a happy one in which they play baseball, volleyball, soccer or ping-pong. Often they sit under the big pine tree in the garden and listen to stories or play the Korean game of "Yute."

By the summer of 1953 the number of CCF-owned or affiliated orphanages had increased to twenty-three; dozens more were pleading for aid. In these Homes, over 4,000 youngsters were being cared for, but the end of CCF's Korean growth was not yet in sight.

During this period, in the little southern village of Bosung Woop, there lived a good Christian woman named Mrs. Park Yung Bai. Here, as near the larger metropolitan areas, the countryside was swarming with frightened starving children. Looking out over the rolling valley from her window one day she saw twelve ragged tots clambering in the trees of her peach orchard. She found that they had not eaten in days and were famished. Soon she had established these youngsters comfortably in her farmhouse as the nucleus of what later became the Baek Ship Ja Home. As the number of children increased to almost one hundred, her means were stretched to the breaking point. Here, too, CCF workers soon contacted her and Dr. Clarke was notified of the need. They were quickly brought into the "CCF fold."

Perhaps one of the most unusual and interesting of the Homes established just prior to the cease-fire is the Ankara

Korean waifs searching a garbage can.

A world at war and in turmoil for two generations left its residue of refugees and orphaned children.

Refugees in the Near East, *left below.*
War-blasted "homes," Southern Italy, *right below.*

C.C.F.'s children in Finland.

C.C.F. has sought to be a good neighbor to the needy children of the world.

Happy, healthy children of the Sinde Mission Home, Southern Rhodesia.

C.C.F.'s affiliate, Inst. S.O.S. Kinderdorf, a fairyland village.

Great help from a former "great house," in Borneo.

German children at the Grosses Deutsches Reichwaisenhaus in Braunsweig, a C.C.F. affiliate founded before Columbus discovered America.

Kindly American Sponsors have "adopted" children.

Rope-skipping—an international sport—at Co-Nhi-Vien Tin Lanh, South Viet Nam.

These little chatters were once foundlings, in Hong Kong.

They have befriended—and many have even visited their "adoptees."

India's Alwaye Settlement serves depressed and fortunate alike.

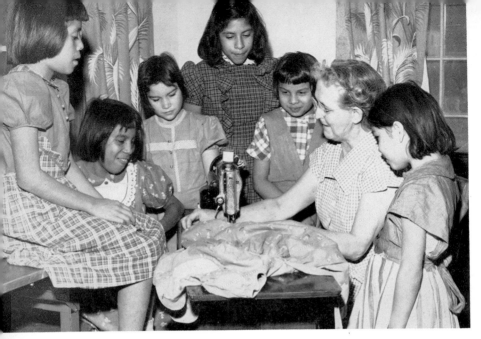

Six little "first Americans" learn to sew in a C.C.F.-affiliated Mission project.

And as near as home—in The Americas, North and South.

Boys at the Instituto Alvaro Rus in Rio de Janeiro learn mechanics as well as academics.

Japanese babies at the Fujo Kai, in the shadow of Mt. Fuji.

Sponsors have been "long distance Aunties" and "Uncles," "brothers" and "sisters," "mothers" and "fathers."

Attractive refugee children in Lebanon.

Korean youngsters, proud of their school uniforms and eager to learn.

They have helped provide schooling.

Pakistani boys and girls learning from the ground up.

Children at the C.C.F. Lutheran affiliated Home in Bethlehem help out.

Yet everywhere the children themselves share simple responsibilities and play is a must.

Italian girls play with this collection of miniature dolls and dishes.

A Middle School Class in C.C.F.'s Children's Garden, Hong Kong, receive their diplomas.

An increasing number of sponsors are seeing their "adoptees" through not only grade and highschool but also through college.

A children's library at the Kama Kura Hockuen, a C.C.F. affiliate in Japan.

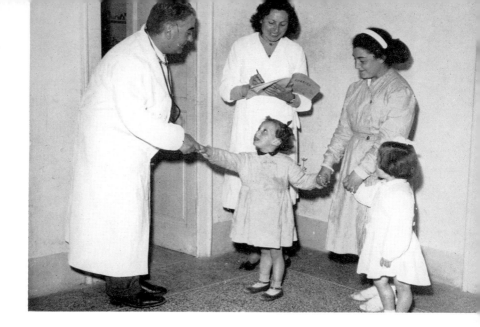

In addition to C.C.F.'s own hospital in Hong Kong and its Pusan Health Home, scores of small clinics and dental chairs are maintained in its own and affiliated Homes. *(Top)* The Casa Materna in Italy. *(Center)* The Instituto Paulo Cesar in Brazil. *(Bottom)* C.C.F. Hospital, Hong Kong.

Hong Kong Boy Scouts and Girl Guides and their sponsors.

4-H is a growing movement—and Boy Scouts would be recognized anywhere in C.C.F. Homes, from Macao to Jamaica.

Pakistani Girl Guides at St. Faith's adapt the uniform to their own pretty dresses.

Asia's first drum majorettes and band, Orphans Home of Korea,
are top performers and earn steadily for "home."

The Three Wise Men winsomely celebrate Christmas at Elizabeth
Saunders Home.

Sponsors send security and warmth to once-scorned children in C.C.F.'s affiliate, the McKean Leprosy Colony in Thailand.

Love for faraway sponsors lights up these children of C.C.F.'s Taichun Home for the Blind.

A City of Children, C.C.F. Children's Garden, Hong Kong: C.C.F. and its American and other contributors have built this little town on one of the bays of Hong Kong's new territories. Nearly 70 cottages (100 is the goal) house over 800 children and their house mothers.

Clarke Junior College is a gift, along with Bott Children's Home, from C.C.F. and American sponsors, to help initiate a professional training program for workers in children's institutions in Japan.

Children's Garden located in the village of Suwon just south of Seoul. The name "Ankara," for the capital of Turkey, is due to the kindness of a Turkish brigade which was stationed nearby at that time. Mr. Ji Tong Ik found one homeless orphan wandering near the camp on a chilly wintry night. He put the boy into a worn army tent to keep warm. The Turkish soldiers gathered around to watch and were soon contributing food and equipment of their own. In a short while, the villagers, hearing of the project, began bringing more children. Thus did the Ankara Children's Garden grow. The Turks contributed materials for permanent buildings to accommodate the youngsters, while the older boys of the orphanage supplied much of the labor to erect the structures.

Eventually seventeen acres of land were purchased through a collection taken at the Turkish encampment. This proved to be prime farm land and was soon supplying the children's hungry mouths with barley, rice, vegetables and peaches. Some baby chicks were contributed and soon the children developed a profitable poultry business. The soldiers continued to take such delight in the children that they also gathered some old musical instruments together and the nucleus of an orphanage band was under way. Today, a 30-piece ensemble composed of both girls and boys turns out some very harmonious sounds. In the year 1961, the Brigade, now back in Turkey, was still sending several truckloads of canned goods per year.

CCF's work soon became so extensive that the orphanages began to specialize in children with particular problems. In several homes, for example, work was being devoted to care for the blind. In others, the children of leprous parents received care. In one Home, youngsters showing a musical talent were educated and sheltered. And in one of CCF's most extensive pieces of work, a Korea-wide organization, the Mei Sil Whoi, the children and widows of Christian workers are cared for. Many of the youngsters are the orphans of Christian martyrs of the War. At no time prior to 1950 and 1951 had the Communists more thoroughly shown their hatred of Christianity (at no prior time, at least, for the eyes of the Western world). A conservative estimate states that at least 500 pastors and Salvation Army officers were brutally "liquidated." The widows elected Mrs. Kim Dong Sook, herself the widow of a minister, as their superintendent. The name of the organization, Mei Sil Whoi, was chosen because it signified "Precious Fruit Society." When I asked this courageous woman why such a name was designated, she replied, "We were determined that the fruits of our husbands' labors should not be in vain!"

CCF's staff helped find some work for the mothers and children. Today, they are engaged in a number of enterprises which contribute toward their support. Some of the mothers embroider, make clothing; others knit and crochet; others are occupied in remaking much of the old clothing sent overseas by the American churches. It is an inspiration to visit and see these wonderful ladies working together in their cutting, stitching, patching, so that others throughout Korea will benefit.

Another orphanage helped by our United States soldiers is the Po Wha Bo Yook Won. Bombs scored a direct hit on its buildings, originally located in Seoul. Many children were injured and killed. The men of the 7th Division, 17th Infantry Regiment, took these youngsters in their arms and loaded them in their trucks, transporting them to the little village of Kumju-ri, just outside Pochun. One large man, a sergeant, wept openly as a three-year-old girl died in his arms. The trucks brought the children to some abandoned farm houses and there they stayed through the bitter winter of late 1950 and early 1951. Through CCF sponsors, the children were fed, clothed and cared for. Eventually, additional funds helped the Orphanage to erect adequate stone buildings as dormitories, classroom buildings and a chapel. Even now on almost any day of any week, should you visit Po Wha Bo Yook, you would probably meet an American GI romping with the youngsters or holding one of the babies in his arms.

One of the most excruciating aspects of the War and its aftermath in Korea, however, is the "Kuji Boy." This is the boy that still wanders the streets of Pusan, Seoul, Taejon and Taegu in the year 1961—eight years after the Panmunjom Armistice. This is the story of Lee Soo Sung, the Pusan shoe-shine boy, whose mother and father died so long ago he can't remember them. It is the story of eight-year-old Shin Heung Koo. He only remembers that he was born on the 14th. Which month, he does not remember. Neither does he remember where he was born.

Heung Koo's father, a worker at the Seoul Railroad Station, died when the boy was a baby. His mother perished in the bitter winter of 1950. About the day he became a complete orphan, he faintly remembers that this happened in a small shack along a tiny stream somewhere in Seoul. Then he was thrown into the whirlwind of the bitter world. He started then as a beggar boy at the South Gate. This lasted about two months. One day he was picked up by a middle-aged man to work as a chore-boy buying charcoal and running errands from early morning to late at night. One day he came home too late, and his master beat him till his legs bled, and then pushed him out the door. His life as a beggar boy began again. He slept wherever his day ended—in a culvert—under a refuse can—usually somewhere in the vicinity of South Gate or the Railroad Station.

Out of his scanty earnings as a beggar, he had to pay "protection" to a man called "the ringmaster." Sometimes this amounted to 100 Hwan, sometimes 50 Hwan (1,000 Hwan equals $1.00 at the present rate). If he could not collect this tribute for the "ringmaster," his eyes were blackened or his nose bloodied. He was just one of 3,000 beggar-boys still roaming the streets of Seoul.

CCF has made many efforts to save these youngsters from such a life. At first, in late 1953 it was estimated that there were close to 100,000 of these youngsters roaming the streets. They wandered singly or in gangs. They became adept at petty thievery. CCF's Director in Korea, Mr. William Henry, tells of the way they attacked him on the streets—an experience of many pedestrians on Seoul Streets. "As I came out of the downtown office, a ragged boy stepped up to me and said 'hey!' I thought he wanted some money and was reaching into my pocket to give him some, when he waved a dirty rag in my eyes. Just then, I felt the pressure of a second boy against my chest. Realizing I was being attacked, I pushed the lad down. As I did so, my wallet and pen fell from his hand to the ground. He scrambled to his feet and the two beggars took to their heels. Many of them are far more expert than this, however."

The tragic fact of expert child-criminals has been attested by many G.I.'s and others. Yet, one must understand, too, their utter rejection by society and the hunger that drives them. W. Neill Thornton related such stories too, on a recent trip to Korea. "One cold morning," he wrote, "last January, a small child stood on a street corner in Taegu. With cup in hand, he begged money from American servicemen. He was clad in a wornout pair of summer shorts, a burlap bag, which substituted for a jacket and a pair of canvas shoes. His ragged clothing failed to offer protection against the winter wind.

"This was Kim Chun Moh, age eleven, who had no home or family ties whatsoever. Both of his parents died along the refugee trail during the early days of the Korean conflict—in the bitter winter of 1950. Now his body was covered with a skin disease. Open sores marked his face and arms." This boy, however, could write a happier outcome to his life.

"Today, thanks to American servicemen," wrote Mr. Thornton, "and other generous Christian donors, Kim is leading a happy normal life. He was picked up from the street corners by three American soldiers, taken to an Army compound where he was fed, washed and clothed. He was then given a home at an orphanage in Taegu (a Home that CCF now helps to support). This orphanage was started by our American troops who, out of the generosity of their hearts, have given $25,000,000 from their meagre pay to help such institutions in Korea."

Many CCF workers have also taken a keen interest in helping these youngsters. One of these earnest people, is a young Methodist missionary named Jack Theiss. Greatly disturbed by the rootlessness of these boys, he began visiting their hangouts in and around Seoul. As they cooked their stews in the beaten cans from refuse pits, he squatted and conversed with them. Progress was not too rapid at first. These youngsters, through bitter experience, trusted no one. Nevertheless, he influenced one after another with his sincerity. Without assistance at first, he undertook to clothe, feed and house them. As the number of boys grew, he received permission from the Methodist Mission Board to build a camp for them. Soon he had erected a large tent on the southerly slope of Mountain 57 outside the city. An elderly minister lent a hand, and with the aid of some friendly G.I.'s, two quonset huts were eventually put up. The boys were taught to use their time profitably in planting vegetable gardens and a rice paddy. In addition, they have displayed remarkable skills in helping to construct a large new wooden dormitory. But most important, they have learned that they are worthwhile persons and that there are those who really care about them, including almost a hundred Americans who have "adopted" them through CCF.

One of these tragic youngsters is Park Jyung Man. He is nine, although he does not remember his birthday. He was born in the village of Yosoo. His right eye is still badly infected because of years of bad food and unsanitary conditions. His father was a farmer. Jyung Man told me, "I dimly remember my father making straw rope in back of our house, but I guess I was only four at the time." His father died soon after that of an unknown disease; then his mother became a prostitute and disappeared. "How did you get to Seoul?" I asked the youngster. "My brother and I climbed aboard a train and hid under a seat after mother ran away. When we arrived in Seoul, my brother told me, 'Wait here,' and then left me. He never came back." In May of 1960 he was found by Reverend Verent Mills and brought to Angels' Haven, the name of the new Home started by Missionary Jack Theiss. He is better now, but he still is unsettled. "What do you want to be when you grow up?" I asked him in late 1960. "Anything," was his reply. "What is your hobby?" "I don't know," he said, "anything."

Abandoned by desperate parents, orphaned by bitter trials, wandering aimlessly—the stories of these youngsters seem unbelievable, yet they are all too real. The Christian Science Monitor, in a 1954 article, described such an abandoned child: "In one recent case, a Protestant missionary found a little girl tied by her leg to a tree in the woods, apparently left there by desperate parents or relatives!"

In Chongju, the work of the Presbyterians was upset by the war. Through funds provided by CCF, their Home for children had been founded by Dr. and Mrs. Harry J. Hill in 1945 after the Japanese had left. At the time, Mrs. Hill was doing Bible teaching in the region when she discovered a group of beggar boys kicking what looked like a rag doll. She interrupted their game abruptly when she heard a tiny cry from the "doll." It turned out to be a month-old infant girl, dressed in rags who had apparently been abandoned in the field. Her heart went out to the baby as she gazed into its wizened face. This tiny bit of life was the nucleus for the Chongju Homes which CCF operates.

Her next discovery was a blind girl whom she found stumbling in the streets of the city. The child had run away from a wine merchant to whom she had been sold for a few Hwan by her parents. Learning that blind children are considered "worthless" in the Far East, she determined to do something for them also. From these meagre beginnings grew the Chongju Home for Blind Children, as well as the Chongju Home for Boys. These children, during the Korean War, were evacuated by "Operation Kiddie-Car," but were repatriated in 1954.

Visiting the Blind Home in late 1960, I was deeply impressed by the things that Reverend and Mrs. Spencer and their fine staff are doing to train these youngsters. I watched them as they went through calisthenics, operated knitting machines, ran a small farm, and even played baseball—all without sight! Slowly these people are teaching the Koreans that blind people are not worthless and that if they are given an opportunity they will prove themselves productive and worthy citizens. In equal competition with sighted children, some of these Chongju Home children have even proven that they are superior in certain national tests!

To meet the ever-increasing need, a large Home for blind children is also owned and operated by CCF in Pusan. It was built and donated by the Hancock Foundation to Christian Children's Fund in 1956.

One of the venerable leaders of Christian orphanages work is K. S. Oh, M.D., whose life history reads like adventure fiction. Imprisoned many times under the Japanese because of his interest in the Korean Independence Movement of 1919, his nobility was of such caliber that the Japanese bestowed re-

lease on him rather than execution. Working at that time
with Mr. Kim Pyung Chan, as well as Dr. and Mrs. Horace
Underwood, he helped to found the Seoul Children's Home.
Under tremendous handicaps they purchased a small farm
outside the city in Anyang. There, cottage style dormitories
were built. Eventually workshops for the training of growing
boys and girls were introduced so that they might learn skills
for a livelihood.

During World War II the going was extremely difficult, and
the Home often faced the necessity of closing. The Japanese
continually knocked on its doors with unreasonable demands
for food and taxes.

In 1947, Christian Children's Fund began helping. Things
greatly improved after this, but in 1950 came the invasion
of the Communists from the North. At the first capture of
Seoul, Dr. Oh was taken and sentenced to death because of
his association with Americans in his work. He was put in
prison, but just five days before his scheduled execution, the
U.N. Forces recaptured Seoul, saving his life.

Dr. Oh's first act, upon release from prison, was to rush out
to the orphanage to see if his orphans were safe. He did find
them safe and well, although many windows had been shattered by bursts of nearby shells. There were other damages to
the property as well, so his next act was to sit down and write
to Dr. Clarke. "Please send a shipment of plastic glass," he
pleaded. He also listed other desperate needs.

No sooner had the consignment been sent from Richmond,
however, than Seoul fell once more to the enemy. This time,
when the fall of the city was imminent, U.N. Army officials,
remembering his imprisonment and near-execution, insisted
that he leave. Dr. Oh with his one hundred children was
flown in the mass evacuation "Operation Kid-Lift" to Cheju
Island. There they remained until after Seoul was recaptured
and finally held permanently by U.N. Forces.

Dr. Oh was the first to return when he hurried back to the Home at Anyang. The orphanage this time was in ruins. But the good earth was still there and he immediately laid plans for spring planting. Thus, all through the summer of 1952, fields of cabbage, barley, turnip and onions and many other crops were planted. These crops were flourishing by the time the children returned in the fall. CCF quickly assumed full responsibility for the erecting of all new cottages, thus inaugurating the first cottage-plan institution in South Korea.

Dr. Oh began gathering materials together for rebuilding. Then, during the summer and early fall, he brought some of the older children from Cheju who helped the builders clear the rubble and wield the hammers and shovels. One after another the neat little cottages went up—the workshops—the kindergarten—the chapel. As room was made available, the children were slowly brought back from Cheju to fill one cottage after another until everyone was finally home again.

No account of CCF's work in Korea would be complete without mention of the remarkable Sae Dol Home in Pusan. There with the aid of American sponsors, Mrs. An Um Jun, the energetic little Korean superintendent, has literally carved an orphanage and farm in the hillside. She and her faithful husband have personally carried hundreds of rocks, laid thousands of bricks, and erected many buildings to create a fairyland home for her children. Her motto has always been "I must put up one more cottage before I die!" She hasn't died yet and the cottages are still going up.

Undoubtedly the most forlorn of all the tragic children are the tiny babies who have been abandoned. Even in 1961 these infants were being abandoned at a phenomenal rate. At least ten a day are being left on doorsteps in Seoul, and six a day in Pusan. Just after the War, the situation was considerably worse. Then the rate was twenty a day or more. During the winter of 1952, the weather was particularly cold around the

city of Suwon. Mrs. Chung Ui Soon was employed at the City
Hall at that time and there she sadly learned at first hand of
the unhappy plight of abandoned tots. They were left on the
City Hall steps by the score, given up by mothers who had
no means left to feed them. There was no foundling home
and certainly City Hall had no facilities to feed these starving
babies. So Mrs. Chung opened her own home to them. Soon
every nook and cranny was filled with infants. She even
took in some five-year-olds and six-year-olds. She could not
resist, for the snow-filled streets were bitter cold.

However, Mrs. Chung was soon scraping the bottom of
the barrel. When her purse was empty, she prayed, "Oh, Lord,
help these babies you have sent me!" The Lord quickly answered by means of the Eighth Bomber Wing of the U.S. Air
Force. A major, whose name is unknown, soon was knocking
at the door with the first bundle of food and clothing. The
help multiplied after that. Through the combined efforts of
the Eighth Bomber Wing and the Korean Civil Assistance
Corps, the present Home was purchased. Today, of course,
these babies receive the love of over three-score Americans
who have "adopted" them through CCF.

These good Americans wrote in by the thousands, their
letters often bringing tears to the eyes of the Richmond staff.
Wrote one:

Dear Dr. Clarke:
 My husband gave his life in Korea. He wrote me of the children that he fed. One of the packages that had been returned
to me unopened was an Easter basket he requested I send
to him, for a little boy he was teaching to speak English.
 He never saw his son, born a month after he was killed. I
would like to "adopt" a little Korean boy, for I think somehow
it would make up for what he has missed. If I have to give
up something to send ten dollars a month for him, it will be
even more meaningful to me.

Are there any babies in the orphanages? My son is two months old, and I could send his clothes to his Korean brother. And then when little Tommy is old enough to write and understand, they could be friends—for they would have much in common.

Please tell me about the orphanages and what I can do.

Sincerely yours,
(Name withheld)

There were, of course, hundreds of American missionaries who worked day and night to rescue these children from certain death. There were the families of the Underwoods, the Appenzellers, descendants of the two original Protestant missionaries to Korea during the 1880's. There were also brave men and women, men like Dr. Charles Sauer, a Methodist who had dedicated almost forty years to the cause of Korean betterment. Dr. Sauer has seen much hardship and privation in his service for his beloved people. Severely persecuted by the Japanese, he also has suffered at the hands of the Communists. During November of 1960, Dr. Sauer's home was attacked by angry "students" undoubtedly under the influence of Communist machination. Fortunately, he and Mrs. Sauer, warned that they were about to be kidnapped, escaped in the nick of time to the Bando Hotel in downtown Seoul. The "students," angered by this frustration, broke into the Methodist compound, broke all of the windows in the Sauer residence and then smashed their way through the doors. Dr. Sauer took me on a "conducted tour" of the damage. The destruction was senseless. Bibles were torn to shreds, missionary records were in tatters, dishes were shattered, doors were in splinters, sheets were ripped, beds crushed, tables demolished, books cut and torn. Hardly anything was salvageable.

"Why?" I asked. "These folks were saying that Dr. Underwood, as president of Yonsei University, and I as Chairman of the Board have been unfair," he said simply. "But this

wasn't done by the Korean people. It was inspired by others."
As though to prove this, for the words were barely out of his
mouth, there was a knock at the door. There stood a delegation of some of Seoul's leading citizens. "We are so sorry—
so ashamed," said their spokesman. "You have always been
our best friend. Here is a gift we have collected to show our
esteem." The man handed Dr. Sauer a generous gift of money
that had been donated out of genuine poverty. Dr. Sauer and
thousands like him the world over are regarded as the truly
"un-ugly Americans."

To Korea in the year 1960 went loving concern for 12,500
children from their American sponsors. To Korea, through
CCF channels went tangible proof of such concern in American dollars—one million of them—for the purpose of binding
up the children's wounds.

This may very well be the hope of Korea's future and the
future of the weary world. As Dr. Daniel Poling has put it,
"Perhaps it is to this future, this prophetic future, that orphan
adoption and the support of homes for the orphaned, this
people-to-people enterprise, contributes. It was the Master
Baby-lover of the world Himself who said, 'A little child shall
lead them!'"

NINE

Love Is a Many-Splendored Work

In the spring of 1951, Dr. Clarke's eyes turned again 2,000 miles to the south of Korea. There in the many-mountained city of Hong Kong the refugees from Red China were surging in. At first the British Colonial Government had welcomed them. These skilled folk from the mainland represented eager hands and vigorous backs to pick up the pieces left by the Japanese. During its occupation by the sons of Nippon, the city had virtually died. In 1941, 1,600,000 had poured into the city, but by 1945, 1,000,000 of these had starved to death or had been driven back into the mainland by privations too rugged to bear. Now they were coming back and the English smiled. Soon, however, British pleasure turned to alarm. There seemed no end to this human stream of misery.

As the Reds drove southward in the spring and fall of 1949, the key cities of Shanghai and Canton collapsed. The roads were black with refugees who poured over the eighteen-mile land frontier into the New Territories (leased to Britain in 1898) and over the Boundary into the Peninsular-city of Kowloon. Then by junk or sampan they sailed across the narrow strait to Victoria on the island of Hong Kong. By early 1951,

99

it was estimated that 2,500,000 of them had crushed in. They overflowed the dwellings and slept in the streets. They built up the wall-like hillsides, clinging like mountain goats. Out of the 391 square miles of valleys and hills, only about twelve square miles are truly habitable. The British took stronger security measures. They stretched a wire fence along the border from Deep Bay to Starling Inlet hoping to seal off the human flood. They erected watchtowers at strategic points along the frontier. They placed floodlights and searchlights at frequent intervals so that the nighttime border would be as bright as day. But somehow people continued to slip through. Policemen were supplied with watchdogs and regular patrols were instituted along the fence. The authorities set up roadblocks in an attempt to pick up any who might slip by the guards at the border. But the refugees soon resorted to the sea. With 600 square miles of water around Hong Kong, and a barren 500 mile coastline, there were opportunities galore to land unseen, by night. CCF was already there waiting to help with food and clothing for them and their babies.

Christian Children's Fund had been operating in Hong Kong since 1939 when Dr. Clarke had sent funds to Fanling Babies' Home and other orphanages and where American sponsors "adopted" their first Hong Kong infants. Soon thereafter, of course, Pearl Harbor was bombed and the Japanese moved into many Pacific strongholds. Hong Kong was one of them. Miss Mildred Dibden, then superintendent, kept a careful diary of the privations through which she went under the Japanese occupation. Her December 8th entry was the first of the four-year nightmare. She wrote in the black-out dimmed light. "First sight of Japanese soldiers marching past the house. I went down to interview the Japanese officer who spoke English. He asked whether I knew where the cables were. I answered that I was a nurse and knew nothing about military measures. He impressed the importance of staying indoors. Anyone seen outside the Home would be shot.

"They started looting and soon found the cases of sweet milk which they dashed on the ground to break open, then scrambled for the tins. I also scrambled and managed to fill my overalls twice over. They were too surprised to stop me— thought it was a fine joke and finished by helping me collect a few.

"One soldier was very brutal. He drove one of the nurses downstairs at the end of his bayonet. He thrust the bayonet at me when I tried to follow. He forced her into the school room.

"The start of a night of terror. Every ten or twenty minutes the soldiers visited upstairs. The babies, partly dressed for the night, were left, many of them uncovered. Nurses crouched in a corner of the small babies' room. Ruth and I went around and covered some of the babies. They were all very quiet, as if they knew something was wrong and were too frightened to cry. Could not find enough blankets in the dark; the soldiers had taken our two lamps and the electricity was cut off. Gave each worker a baby to hold to keep that many warm.

The soldiers incessantly clumping upstairs after us. The sound of their boots strikes terror into the hearts of us all, and as the torch light comes around the corner of the doorway, the young nurses and amahs huddle behind us, each pushing and struggling, afraid to be on the outside in case they will be the next to be dragged off by the soldiers. Had a tremendous blow on the head with the butt end of a rifle because I was in a soldier's way and was trying to save a nurse. Occasional visits to us to drag off one or another. I had to continually cry out 'Mind the babies, don't kill the babies!' Pitch dark and very cold.

"A young nurse dodged behind a baby's cot. He kicked over

the cot, baby and all. It fell to the floor with a crash before I could save it. The baby died later.

"We prayed earnestly for protection and then the idea came to me. 'Shout,' I cried. 'All shout.' And we did. We just screamed with all our might. It relieved our feelings and it made the soldiers run. They ran as if the whole British force was behind them. The soldiers had used our mattresses as couches. They were stained with jam, sweet milk and other tinned food. There were tins everywhere, some empty, some half empty and others just opened to see what was inside and thrown away."

As soon as the soldiers had fled, the staff set bravely to work to repair what damage they could. But there were dour prospects ahead. Excerpts from Miss Dibden's diary throughout the next four years indicated that after the initial onslaught of rape and brutality the Japanese often showed compassion and genuine love for the children. But war being monstrously evil, the suffering was nevertheless great.

Her diary reported:

"March 14, 1942. There is no milk for the tiny babies. Ground rice and water proves to be slow starvation for them. It is only a matter of days before we have to take them out and bury them.

"May 5. Several children have died this week.

"July 11. A party of friends arrived from Hong Kong with permits to take us to the French Hospital. I am on a stretcher.

"June 2, 1943. We have taken in nine new children in four days. All a pathetic sight, on the border of starvation.

"July 25. Six of the nine new arrivals have died. It is better so.

"Aug. 13. Cholera suspected in the Home.

"Aug. 14. Our landlord died of the cholera today.

"Sept. 9. The epidemic seems to be over.

"Oct. 12. Gift of 1,000 yen from Chinese gentlemen.

"Dec. 25. Christmas morning. We managed a few second-hand toys and odd pieces of cloth for a Christmas tree.

"Aug. 9, 1944. Our clothes are patched again and again. Can they possibly go through another year?

"Feb. 14, 1945. The starvation of the people everywhere is pitiful to see.

"May 9. Germany's unconditional surrender is in the Japanese paper.

"Aug. 10. News that Russia has entered the Pacific War. What now?

"Aug. 12. Japan has surrendered!

"Aug. 18. Riots starting.

"Aug. 27. The Japanese Government, with tons of rice in store, is sharing it out amongst charitable institutions.

"Sept. 1. Canadian boys! How great to see them on duty.

"Sept. 7. We are safe at last, no more to fear. We ate our dinner in an elegant room of the great Kowloon Hotel. I am leaving for England with the Home in CCF hands. Supplies will be sent out, milk and chocolate for the children, tin foods for the staff. Our God has brought us through deep waters."

Upon the conclusion of the Pacific War, a new Far Eastern Office was set up by Dr. Clarke. The Fanling Home's grounds were chosen as the most strategic spot, and a tiny garden house was selected as the office building. Here, in 1947, Reverend Erwin Raetz and a small staff began the coordination of funds and mail for what eventually became a vital nerve center of widespread aid.

One of the first things that needed doing was to assist the many abandoned babies. Hundreds of them came through Fanling and were cared for there or processed for other Homes. By 1949 and 1950, the Government was reporting between ten and fifteen thousand babies abandoned in Hong Kong every year. Eighty per cent of these were doomed to almost certain death. Despite the herculean efforts of missionaries and agencies like CCF it was physically impossible to cushion this Niagara of need. Nevertheless, CCF was even then aiding 1,200 children in six separate Homes.

Surveying the field, Dr. Clarke's visit in 1950 showed the overwhelming odds that CCF faced. It was at this time that Mr. Raetz resigned and Verent Mills was appointed Overseas Director. When all of Hong Kong's flat land had been occupied, squatters built flimsy shacks up the hillsides. Every ravine was crammed with them; fashioned from cardboard, burlap sacking on shaky wood frames, flattened gasoline cans, their multitude staggered the imagination. Quickly, Mills ordered that CCF set up an emergency food and clothing depot at Rennies Mill Camp. Thousands were to be fed and cared for here, and hundreds of children "adopted" before the need for this work ceased in early 1961.

By 1950, in downtown Kowloon and Hong Kong the teeming populace had taken up residence on the streets. Wherever he looked Dr. Clarke saw the flimsy shacks, the clumsy shelters under the balconies, the huddled children on the filthy pavement, the rickety fire traps on the roofs. He saw the squatter towns containing hundreds of thousands—each with its brothels, its opium dens, its gambling houses. He saw tiny abandoned children exposed daily to these raw evils.

Home after home was built or enlarged to care for some of these innocent pawns of war and distress. At Taipo Market, the teeming Wanchai District, and at St. Christopher's Home in the New Territories, as well as many another, Americans gladly "adopted" and helped them.

But still the population grew. Government and citizen looked on in alarm. Something had to be done. However, the official hands were forced on Christmas Night, 1953. On that fateful eve the greatest fire in Hong Kong history swept through the squatter settlement in the Shek Kip Mei district. Forty-five acres of tinder-box dwellings went up in a bomb-like fire. The next morning the smoke from the smouldering ruins hovered above 60,000 displaced people. The Government's plans for a $250,000,000 housing re-settlement project had been on the drawing board for many months. Now haste was required to put a roof above 60,000 heads. Fifty-three days later, fire-evicted tenants moved into the first of the re-settlement houses, known as "H-Blocks." In 1958, the Government could report that $70,000,000 had been expended to house 200,000 homeless. Accommodations for 200,000 more were envisioned. In these compact seven-storey cement-and-steel structures, each family was provided with a tiny cubicle, 120 feet square. True, this is small by western standards, but it has a tremendous advantage over the paper shacks it replaces in Hong Kong. The new home proved to be fireproof, clean and dry. It provided electric lights, communal bathrooms and rooftop playgrounds. It guaranteed better health by supplying sewage and garbage disposal; and in each H-Block was a small but efficient clinic to care for emergency medical requirements. Most important from the standpoint of CCF work were the rooftop play and study areas. Here in early 1954, the first of the CCF-Rooftop projects for children commenced. By 1960, between three and four thousand "rooftop" children had been "adopted" by sponsors. These children received supplementary help for meals, clothing, school supplies and other necessities.

Thousands of children were not so lucky. Three children of Lee Kim Wong were visited by CCF Board member Dr. Daniel Poling in the summer of 1954. In describing their experience, he said, "Their father had been for fourteen years a pilot on the Chinese commercial airways. Then his wife died and he resigned his position to keep the family together. He was a man of great intelligence and education and became a correspondent on a Shanghai newspaper that also had a Canton edition. When the Communists captured the city, they at once arrested forty-seven editors and correspondents. The father was seized. His weeping children stood at the door and watched him taken away by four Communist soldiers.

"Two days later, a soldier returned and told the eldest child that if her father was to have food, she must bring his daily rice and vegetables. The 'People's Government' considers all prisoners of the people as unworthy of the 'people's food,' she was informed. For two months the sixteen-year-old, with her oldest brother, carried the food to the great prison across the river from Canton.

"One morning the children were told that their father had gone way. They hurried home in the glad hope that they might find him there. They were disappointed. They learned from a neighbor that there would be a mass execution of the editors and correspondents that afternoon—a public execution and all were required to be present. Even the grade schools were dismissed for such 'horror events.' In trembling fear, the five motherless children hurried the four miles and a half to the mass execution. But they were too late—it was finished."

Dr. Poling met the children a few months later in Hong Kong. They were among the tens of thousands that had been burned out in Shek Kip Mei. "The sobbing child of twelve told me how her sister had led them through the milling crowd until they reached the bodies. They searched until they found their father. The top of his head was gone. 'I am sure he knew us,' said the child wistfully, 'because he moved when we came.' Muscular reactions could explain that. It was a good thing that the child could talk about it as she did—even childhood must have release from grieving. But I had no answer for her question, 'Why did they kill my daddy? He was a good daddy.'"

In the fall of the following year, Dr. Clarke made another quick visit to Hong Kong. Visiting Victoria Island, he described what he saw of the conditions in Wanchai, the now-famous "Suzie Wong" area. "Here," he said, "less than fifteen minutes from the center of downtown Hong Kong are roughly 2,000 people existing to every acre. Twenty per cent of them are suffering from tuberculosis. More than half the children do not get enough sleep, because those who are fortunate enough to have beds must sleep three and five to a bed. Others sleep thirty to thirty-five on the floor of a single room. I saw one little girl huddled hopelessly on the water-soaked pavement in a driving rain. As I traveled along this same thoroughfare I saw more and more tiny figures hunched against the cold walls for protection. Hunger is their constant companion. The majority of these youngsters are receiving only about 50 per cent of their regular calorie requirements. Ninety-five per cent of them need dental treatment. One Chinese doctor told me that their little bodies are being ravaged by the poison rampant within them from their badly infected teeth and mouths."

As he surveyed what was being done for them, he contacted missionaries of the Church of England who were constantly going among these forlorn tots searching out the neediest. Joining forces with these earnest people, he turned again to CCF sponsors. Gladly American friends assumed "adoptions" for 200 children in newly established St. James Settlement. They were able to engage the services of a cultured young Chinese woman, Miss Lee Hei Man, a graduate of London University with a degree in sociology. Soon a staff of twelve full-time and six part-time workers was hard at work ministering to these children. A make-shift clinic was established at first, for initial remedy of the great children's dental and medical needs.

Soon Miss Lee and her staff were conducting classes in reading and writing; then came classes in artistic and industrial skills. With good clothes and food, plus care and love, the youngsters quickly filled out and took to their new schedule eagerly.

It was not long before CCF was aiding ten such projects, Homes and settlements. But still the refugee children cried out for aid—thousands of them with nowhere to turn. The pressures of Communism behind them, the ideologies of the Western world surrounding them, the minds of these milling masses were often confused. In 1953 and 1954 the stream of Western missionaries and educators was still coming across the Lowu Bridge into the New Territories. By now, of course, the stream was reduced to a trickle, but still the weary people came.

Dr. Poling, there in 1953, met one such dedicated person out of the hundreds—her name, Miss Annie James. "A New Zealand Presbyterian, for nearly forty years she had been a missionary in South China. When the Communists came in, taking over the hospital of which she was a superintendent, they accused her of complicity in the death of the invalid son of a Communist general.

"Acquitted of that charge, she was held while studies were made of case records in her institution. Later, she was charged with responsibility in the deaths of all who had died in her hospital while she was superintendent. Under this monstrous indictment, she was convicted. But even more appalling, after weeks of mental and psychological torture she 'confessed.' Eventually, she was released from Canton to Hong Kong and is now sufficiently recovered to assume again a responsible position."

Political conflict in Hong Kong is always ready to flare up, but it came to a real blaze on October 1, 1956. This is called the "Double Tenth" by the Nationalists. Some Red sympathizers pulled down the Nationalist flag above one of the newly-erected H-Blocks. British government officials, mindful of the local undercurrent between Nationalists and Reds, ordered the lowering of the flag which had been reflown. Tempers flared, other flags were ripped down, and thousands of Nationalist followers ranged the streets looting and burning. Soon the riot turned from an anti-Red demonstration into an anti-foreigner uproar. Rampaging along Nathan Road, they seized and beat many foreigners, Americans among them. Reverend Norman Turner, now CCF's Hong Kong Director, was saved by police in the nick of time as he took to his heels before a blood-thirsty mob.

Laying violent hands on the automobile of one foreigner, they overturned it with the helpless woman driver inside. Quickly they transformed it into a flaming coffin, and several hours later the wife of the Swiss Consul died of third-degree burns in the hospital. The mob grew as the violence increased until finally authorities sent out spotter planes and the armed forces, supporting the police, used tear and vomit gas to quell the riot. Emergency squads were dispatched into the streets to help the dead and dying. One stretcher-bearer described the horror he saw with lurid detail: "In one place," he recalled, "I found a shoe containing a human foot." When finally brought under control, the riot had caused the death of forty-seven Chinese and foreigners. One hundred stores had been utterly ruined by the looting. Three thousand rioters had been arrested. It was the worst outbreak in Hong Kong since the end of the Japanese War. The English redoubled their security measures, quietly deporting all known ringleaders whether Communist or Nationalist.

Dr. and Mrs. Clarke, visiting the city shortly thereafter, felt that this was a moment to demonstrate what American Christianity stood for. "Wouldn't it be wonderful," said Mrs. Clarke, "if here in this 'showcase of democracy' on the very doorstep of Communism we could do something special!" In considering many possibilities, CCF Board members finally approved "Mrs. Clarke's Dream"—the largest cottage-plan orphanage in the Far East. The first installment of this orphanage was finished in the latter part of 1957—its name, Children's Garden. It quickly became world famous.

I shall never forget my first glimpse of this tremendous operation as I rode across Tolo Harbor in the motor launch "The Lady Clarke." Boy Scouts and Girl Scouts in their trim uniforms were on the pier to greet me. As I looked up this long line of happy youngsters, my eye followed a tremendous panoramic sweep. In the foreground, the neat stone cottages, centering around a playground and a stone chapel. In the background was the new hospital provided for the Home by an anonymous gift. In addition, the Hong Kong Government contributed over $300,000 to this million-dollar project.

These children had been housed in rented buildings up to 1956. With the sharply rising rents, however, this soon became prohibitive. Acting on faith, as well as on the faithfulness of CCF's American friends, Dr. and Mrs. Clarke urged the then Overseas Director, Reverend Verent Mills, to proceed on an ambitious plan. Built of the rock from the hillside in this far-removed part of the New Territories, the sturdy little houses and school rooms were designed to be typhoon-proof. But best of all, each house was to be "home"—the original plan called for 100 of these when finished. In 1960 there were already 68 of them. Each cottage was assigned a housemother, carefully chosen. And in each home was an assorted "family," a pioneering experiment by CCF that paid off. These families consisted of youngsters of every age from toddler to teen—girls and boys—twelve children to a family. A large living-dining room converted to other uses when necessary. The bedrooms each contained two double-decker bunks with double desks and lockers for the four occupants. "Mother" had her room and then there was also the kitchen, Chinese in outline, but modern and sanitary with its white tile and tinted cement floor.

From the moment when the first youngsters from Hong Kong's streets entered Children's Garden, the cottage families vied with one another in planting vines and flower borders. The wide walks were swept clean each day and grassy terraces were kept clean and neat. Then, too, situated as the Children's Garden is on Tolo Bay, there is a wonderful beach for swimming and fishing.

In many a child's eye at Children's Garden, however, there is still the gleam of terror as he remembers what he escaped. Surrounded as he is now by peace and security, he recalls gnawing hunger, hideous nights of death and terror. He remembers the dread word HSIAO MIEH—"deprived of existence."

Foreign experts have estimated, after investigating reports of refugees pouring into Hong Kong, Macao and Formosa, that at least 20,000,000 Chinese have been "deprived of existence" during the past ten years. In addition, there are unquestionably 23,000,000 more who are being "detained" in forced labor camps. It is difficult to visualize this staggering massacre, and oppression, but a tiny microcosm of it can be detected in each child's eyes.

Horrified observers, including photographers from *Time* magazine witnessed a bit of it across the Hong Kong-Kwangtung border in early 1956. There they watched as scores of "peasant landlords" were executed by the "People's Army." Kneeling, and with arms tightly bound, these "capitalists" were shot in the back for their "crime of deviation."

Little wonder that refugees continued to pour out of mainland China into every port possible, coming by the hundreds of thousands. And with them—the children. Although officials strung barbed wire they came by boat. Although the beaches were patrolled by Communist soldiers, they still came through under the cover of night. But for every one succeeding, six died. They stowed away aboard the Red vessels plying the Pearl River. They swam in—or were washed in, dead. Desperation drove them. Death was behind them. Even starvation in Hong Kong was preferable.

Seeking safer ground, the fleeing Chinese did not choose only Hong Kong, however. Many of them escaping with some capital were able to arrive in areas of Southeast Asia where they joined other Chinese who had lived there for generations. Those who were able to, set up rice mills, banks, stores or commerce throughout the whole troubled area. In Thailand it was reliably reported in 1961 that such Chinese controlled nine out of ten of the rice mills. In Vietnam, Laos, Cambodia and the Philippines, the ratio was eight out of ten. In Singapore Chinese accounted for 77 per cent of the total population.

Outnumbering those who are better off, there are the tens of thousands of destitute, starving, ragged, hopeless people. With them came the reports of famine from inside Red China. Crop failures, unprecedented flood conditions, and "calculated starvation" were responsible for the death of millions. In order to force the populace into agricultural communes, the Communists followed a policy of forced rationing. A staff member of CCF, recently escaped from Red China, reported the ration currently in effect. For each "authorized person" who held such a ration card the food supply was:

    2 ounces of pork every ten days
    4 ounces of sugar every month
    10 ounces of soy bean oil monthly
    20 ounces of rice every month (normally, a 2-day supply)

A minimum diet of existence is 1400 calories per day. The ration being allowed by the Red Government was 700 calories per day. Indeed, in many areas, the average person was not even getting that.

One of the inhuman aspects of the "People's Government" is that boats loaded with produce still flow into Hong Kong.

In late 1960, I walked the busy docks of Victoria and watched the boats that fly the Red flag as they unloaded. Bags of rice, crates of apples, vegetables, meat products were piled methodically on the piers. They had all been shipped down the river and past the very mouths of millions who groaned for a crust. The Red policy was apparently to ship such saleable merchandise for gold to be used in purchasing strategic materials in neutral countries of Europe. Millions of Chinese peasants were thus declared expendable.

Meanwhile, however, a great unrest was stirring in Southeast Asia. Nationalism, Communist intrigue, civil war, and overpopulation conspired throughout the fifties to splinter thousands of youngsters from their family trees. It was to this area, during this period, therefore, that Dr. Clarke dispatched Verent Mills and others with offers of additional CCF aid.

TEN

On the Road to Mandalay
and Elsewhere

IN 1954, the long-drawn-out civil war in Indochina burst into
its final explosion. With the Communist drive on the French
forts at Dien Bien Phu in April and May, the conflict came to
an end. On July 21st the lines of demarcation between Com-
munist-held territory and freedom were drawn at the 17th
Parallel. Indochina, by the terms signed at Geneva, was di-
vided into North and South Vietnam, Laos and Cambodia.
Needless to say, the suffering of the people was tremendous.

When the Communists won possession of the rich Red
River delta along with the capital city of Hanoi, 40,000 resi-
dents fled. At the same time at least 400,000 refugees streamed
across the 17th Parallel into South Vietnam. Children were
wounded, abandoned or orphaned by the thousands.

During the eight years of civil war Dr. Clarke had been
sending CCF workers to investigate and to set up an emergency home in the city of Nhatrang. One little six-year-old boy
was typical of the hundreds who were rescued. During the
fierce warfare in his area north of Hanoi, he had stumbled
along the road in the blazing sun. Two days before, all of his
family had been wiped out by the Reds. He had escaped only

114

because his father had sent him out to the garden to gather vegetables and fruit. He hid when he saw the soldiers coming. He had watched with unbelieving eyes as they machine-gunned his mother, father, sisters and brother.

He staggered with hunger and fatigue as he struggled toward Hanoi. He knew that if he kept on the big road long enough he would get away from the men who had burned his house and shot down his family as they were driven out by the flames. His feet were blistered and his head throbbed with the heat, yet he kept on all day in the sun. When it grew dark, he tried to stumble on, for he was afraid of the snakes. Several times his small legs gave way and he fell. Finally he could go only a few feet and then he would fall again. At last he came to a long bridge where he was no longer afraid of snakes. He crawled as close to the rail as he could and tried to keep awake so that no truck would run over him. But he fell asleep anyway.

Suddenly, he heard a man's voice speaking to him and he opened his eyes. The man was putting him on the driver's seat of his truck. Two other men were there with guns. They asked him a lot of questions and he told them about his family being shot down. The men did not look at him while he talked. They were holding their guns and watching the road. He could not sit up any longer. So he lay down beside the driver. He heard the driver say, "Let's take him to that Christian Children's Fund orphanage." He wondered what that was— but his tears felt hot upon his face. He knew his mother, father, sisters and brother would not be there.

There were others who came later: In the following six years there were thousands of others. The Communist gueril-las infiltrated, burned, pillaged, and murdered. More recently there was the Hiep family, just one of many. When the father of the household volunteered, he was given a gun and told to defend his farm. He and his neighbors were soon overwhelmed. Many were ruthlessly butchered. Others, like Mr. Hiep, were buried alive after five days' forced march into the jungle.

And in the wake of this new onslaught, CCF again moved in to care for the survivors. Dr. Clarke publicized their plight among Americans. Over $3,000 was donated to help the Hieps alone, enough to build a home, as well as to feed and educate the children.

In the city of Nhatrang, CCF workers found just the person to superintend the vital work of caring for more lost children. An earnest pastor named Le-van-Thai was enlisted to establish what is now known as the Co-Nhi-Vien-Tin Lanh Home. For the past six years it has cared for hundreds of youngsters, victims of brutal warfare. American sponsors have increasingly shown their concern for these tots by their faithful gifts and letters.

Meanwhile, just across the border was another ancient nation whose way of life was threatened by Communist aggression. Alarmed by the inroads made by Red treachery in its neighboring countries, Thailand proved to be the first of the Southeast Asian nations to accept the American proposal for a united front against such aggression. In September of 1954, it entered into negotiations that laid the early foundations for SEATO. In June of 1956, the headquarters for that body— Southeast Asia Treaty Organization—were dedicated in Thailand's capital city of Bangkok. It soon gained a reputation as the nation most strongly opposed to Communism among all its neighbors. Nevertheless, its needs remained great, and the distress of its children was often bitter. Its proximity to the equator also added certain tropical complications to troubled childhood—one of which was leprosy.

In an inspection trip to this country during that period, Dr. Clarke's representative Reverend V. J. Mills visited the work that had been begun a half-century previously by a Presbyterian missionary. Laboring under terrific odds this clinic and home was performing one of the most effective ministries in all of Asia. Known as the Chiengmai Leprosy Colony, it had its inception under a great saint named James W. McKean. Oddly enough, the colony's history shows that Dr. McKean shares the "founding honors" with a white elephant.

More than fifty years ago, a king in Northern Siam—now Thailand—gave to his eldest son as a coming-of-age present an immense royal white elephant. The beast proved to be, indeed, a "white elephant" in every sense of the word. He was both vicious and dangerous. After killing several of his keepers, he was hobbled and placed on an island in the Maping River below Chiengmai. Here he was so destructive that the island's inhabitants moved away. After the elephant's eventual death, the jungle took over.

Several years passed, and the King's son, who had now succeeded to the throne, became greatly interested in the work of Dr. McKean. Since he admired the missionary so greatly, he asked him one day, "What can I give you for your work that would please you most?" After a moment of thought, the doctor replied, "The Island of the White Elephant." Soon after, he went to the island with eight ragged lepers and there he cleared a place in the jungle where the colony came into being. Thus, say the natives, the kindness of the white doctor and the viciousness of a white elephant founded a Home.

Located 500 miles from the capital city of Bangkok, the Colony has become the greatest Christian enterprise in all Thailand. With its many buildings and cottages it has grown into a small town on the 164 acres of the island surrounded by the Maping River. Just across the bridge which is also the "gate to the Colony," is a smaller compound which accommodates the dormitories and schools of the lepers' "clean" children.

Leprosy, according to pathologists, is not inherited. It can, however, be contagious if contact with a leper is sustained over too long a period. Children who have not contracted the disease would probably get it from their parents unless they were separated.

Finding the financial needs to be overwhelming, Verent Mills wired Dr. Clarke about the circumstances. The Colony soon became a part of CCF's expanding family. As funds from Christian Children's Fund sponsors permitted, the "clean" children were taken from their parents and put in the colony opposite the island. Here these youngsters were also given their own kindergarten and school.

Life, even on the "island of lepers" is more cheerful than one might expect. Here the leprous children, as well as adults have learned to hope. Great advances have been made in retarding or overcoming this ill, now known as "Hansen's Disease." Every effort is made to compensate for the handicaps of wasted or missing portions of the body. The children learn to raise pigs, cows, chickens, ducks as well as other livestock. They also have become adept at tending gardens and fruit trees. They even grow their own mulberry bushes and silkworms. Along with all of this, they have also learned how to fashion bamboo baskets and mats.

One thing that has shown their optimism and fighting spirit is the manner in which they repair their own physical handicaps. One child who had lost a portion of his leg was discovered making a bamboo leg to take its place. Another young man who had lost his fingers fashioned a bamboo "mitt" to slip on the stump of his hand. And all of the children, crippled though they may be by this dread ailment, take active part in games and sports in addition to their studies.

Perhaps one of the most heartening things at the Colony is the way the disease is responding to antibiotic drugs. Complete cures are being effected almost every day. In addition, remarkable surgery is now being performed by Dr. Chinda

Singhanet. After studying the methods of Dr. Paul Brand in India, he has operated on scores of leprosy-damaged hands. Dr. Chinda, along with other physicians who specialize in Hansen's Disease, has discovered that leprosy strikes the hands and feet first, in over 50 per cent of the cases. Crippling paralysis from the disease renders the fingers useless.

Tests and studies also show, however, that although leprosy struck most of the arm and finger muscles, there always seemed to be one set of arm muscles immune to paralysis. Dr. Chinda's surgery on the hands of "his children" involved the transplant of good muscles and tendons to other areas where they could do the work of the paralyzed ones. Grateful youngsters by the score have had their hands "given back" by Chinda Singhanet's surgical skill.

No account of the McKean Colony is complete without the story of Pin. She was discovered in late 1959 by Verent Mills during a tour of inspection. "I laid my hand on the girl's head," he related, "as she sat there on the floor. I thought she was a normal youngster until I looked down. Then I discovered to my dismay that this sweet lass had no feet—they had been 'eaten away' by the disease." Mr. Mills related Pin's story to Dr. Clarke on his return to Richmond. Not long after that, her picture and history appeared in national magazines throughout the United States. People by the hundreds were touched by the poignancy of her expression and by her great need. Several thousand dollars soon came in earmarked for Pin. Much of the money was donated anonymously. But attached to more than one check was a note, "I want to help Pin get new feet." Soon the skilled surgery of Dr. Chinda will make it possible for her to use artificial feet and Pin will walk again, through the kindness of unnamed Americans.

Meanwhile, Karl Marx's dialectic was being chanted far to the south in Singapore. For seven years British and Malayan troops had battled Soviet-inspired guerillas recruited from the

Chinese population. Sporadic attacks on the rubber planta-
tions grew in intensity until the Malayan Government began
in 1954 to deport the troublesome elements. For a time, am-
nesty had been offered to these bloodthirsty intruders if they
came out of hiding. But negotiations in this direction soon collapsed. Chief Minister Tengku Abdul Rahman even offered
carfare home to every Communist terrorist who would surrender. When this offer was refused, government policy stif-
fened against all Red activity. A mutual defense pact was
signed with Thailand to protect their mutual border from
infiltration.

Because of the continual interchange of population as well
as its burgeoning growth, the pressures proved immense in
Singapore. Here a massed and struggling humanity scrabbled
for existence. On an island one-seventh the size of New York's
Long Island, 1,500,000 human beings, speaking a dozen different Asiatic languages and dialects competed for a meager food
supply. Every seven minutes a baby is born. He may be European, Chinese, Malayan, Indian or Eurasian, but he is added
to the melting pot that increases by 50,000 births a year.

Surveying this desperate area in the early fifties, Dr. Clarke
found at least four Salvation Army orphanages courageously
struggling to rescue the hundreds of street waifs who were
homeless and hopeless. Again, CCF sponsors when apprised
of the problems responded with hearty generosity. A cooperative CCF-Salvation Army operation soon made it possible
to "adopt" many more youngsters.

At the same time on Mayala's Penang Island, a unique but
floundering ministry called out for assistance. Known by the
natives as "The House of Light," the St. Nicholas Home for
the Blind had been operating twenty or more years. Some
friends of children, seeing the plight of sightless little ones,
collected enough funds to purchase a two-story stucco building in Penang. There the groping children have learned to

read Braille, to work and even to play underneath the spreading camphor tree in the courtyard. Through CCF sponsors, many extras such as better food, toys, and guidance have been made possible.

To this home one day in the late fifties stumbled Wong Su, a blind girl of eleven. She sobbed out her story to the superintendent: "I was sold as a slave—very cheaply because I was blind. In the darkness I tried hard to earn my rice. But the man who bought me was cruel. I could never avoid his raised hand because I could not see it coming. Sometimes he beat me until I fainted and then he kicked me. I lived in pain and fear most of the time till I wished I was dead. Finally, I ran away. Please take me into your Home and help me." Tears came to the eyes of the staff as they listened. Putting their arms around the child they led her to the place that "became her very own." She is just one of the scores of boys and girls daily helped at the St. Nicholas Home for the Blind.

At the eight other CCF-assisted orphanages in Malaya, there is a wide variety of children. One little girl had lost her home and parents and was living like a small animal on the city street. Another was a slave boy who had run away. A Salvation Army officer had found him huddled in a gutter and brought him to an orphanage. Another had fled in panic from Communist guerillas in the "Bandit country" when his parents were slaughtered before his eyes. Many of the children have seen both mother and father waste away with the dread "white plague" of T.B. All they can bring to the orphanage is their need. Ill-treated and fearful—the doors of the homes swung open and received them.

Also wrestling with Asia's demon of Sovietism is Malaya's western neighbor, Burma. In 1957, Communist terrorists and rebelling Karen tribesmen threatened full revolt. At the same time, Burmese troops struggled with Chinese Communist troops along the northern border. Added to this modern evil arc the older ones of superstition, witchcraft and cannibalism.

In the Burmese village of Tahan near the border of India is one of the newest orphanages assisted by CCF. When Dr. Clarke learned of children's needs here, during July of 1960, he urged the Board to add them to CCF's "international boarding-house." (CCF had been assisting other Burmese homes since 1947.)

In the wild area surrounding the Irrawaddy River dwell the Naga tribes from which most of the orphanage's children come. The most backward of all Burmese people, these primitive folk still feast on human flesh. During recent intertribal warfare, many of the children's parents have been killed and eaten. One horrified youngster had to watch in the flickering firelight, the grisly sight of his captors devouring his father. "I still hear him screaming," he tells the orphanage staff worker who awakens him from an oft-repeated nightmare. Only the love and care of the Tahan Orphanage will eventually remove some of the scars left by such devastating experience. An American sponsor wrote him his first letter recently with the words, "Let me be your 'daddy' now, won't you?" Most of the children have already been "adopted" through Christian Children's Fund.

Just north of the equator, on the shores of the South China Sea are other CCF-sponsored homes. In Sarawak, for example, on the Island of Borneo, CCF operates cooperatively with the Methodists in an orphanage at Sibu. Sarawak, under British control since the late forties, still knows many primitive customs, especially in the back-country. Head-hunting, for instance, while it has ceased to exist as a common practice, has not vanished altogether. Child slavery, on the other hand, is still prevalent. It is estimated that 2,000 children are sold into slavery here every year. Boys often sell at the rate of $100 apiece. Girls are somewhat higher, ranging from $150 to

$200 each. Some of these youngsters, orphaned, abandoned, or sold into servitude, are even forced to become opium runners.

On a 1955 trip to the Sibu Home, Dr. Clarke met Lin Sieh Cing, aged ten. She had been a slave, bought and paid for. Her family had lived in the jungles of that island colony. One day head-hunters attacked her home. Sieh Cing saw both her mother and her father beheaded. She herself was frightfully slashed by the savage warriors. With face and body streaming blood, she was dragged to their village and there she was sold into slavery. At length she ran away and was brought to the orphanage at Sibu.

Here Sieh Cing soon discovered that at least fifteen of the children in the Home were at one time slaves. Most of them were girls—child wives. Such youngsters are ordinarily sold at the ages of five to eight, ostensibly to become wives in the families who bought them; actually, they become slaves to the whole family and work as unpaid servants.

The orphanage was started almost accidentally, in October of 1949. Methodist missionary Mrs. J. A. Pilley was teaching one day in the mission compound when she beheld a sight that made her hair rise. An oversized "mother-in-law" was lashing one of these five-year-old children until the blood ran. Acting from impulse, the missionary wrested the lash from the woman and took the child from her. Officials, finding that the child had suffered a long history of such beatings, "awarded" the youngster to Mrs. Pilley. A bit nonplussed, she willingly took little Hieh Wong Sch into her home. Soon Mrs. Pilley discovered other children who were being abused and neglected. "I could not resist the pleading of their dark eyes," she related. In a short while funds were necessary, for the Pilleys had run out of room. Many local people helped them and not long thereafter a pleasant house was erected.

Today, through the careful nurture of Methodist missionaries, grounds have been made lush with tropical flowers, as well as a vegetable garden bordered by an orchard yielding papaya and other tropical fruit. Through the kindness of American friends, a play yard with swings and a "jungle gym" has been made possible. And of course the children have been "adopted" by CCF sponsors.

"When the Communists drove us out of China," says this devoted couple, "we thought our ministry was finished. But now look," they point to the girls in colorful print dresses and the boys in clean shirts and shorts, "We have a brand-new family!"

One of the areas of most prayerful concern to Dr. Clarke and millions of other Americans, however, is the new-born nation of Indonesia. Situated largely on the islands of Java and Sumatra, this country numbers 84,000,000 people. Headed by its strong-minded chief executive President Sukarno, it is at once both friendly and neutral. In spite of his tolerance of Communists in his government, he has remained somewhat cool toward the nations of the Communist bloc. In 1960, he accepted a $250,000,000 credit from Russia, but steadfastly maintained that he was "neutral." Later in the year, he angered the Communist countries by ordering the deportation of thousands of Chinese "merchants" who were acquiring an iron grip on trade in rural areas. Later he relaxed this mandate provided these Chinese would become naturalized citizens of Indonesia.

With the withdrawal of Dutch support after December 1949, children's homes which formerly had received financial aid were left to flounder. One of these, Salib Putih, on the tropical isle of Java, had been founded by a kindly Dutch Christian named S. A. Van Emerick. He began the work in 1902 when he found some ragged orphans on the streets of Samarang that borders on the Java Sea. Taking them inland to Salatiga he built some primitive shacks, at first, right in the middle of the jungle. Relying on his faith and fortitude he continued to collect hungry waifs and bring them to the orphanage. Slowly he and the older boys built extra dormitories, barns, kitchens and a church. The crowning structure was a hospital that was just being equipped when the Pacific War broke out.

Meinheer Van Emerick watched with a broken heart in 1942 as the Japanese military penetrated the jungle and took over his beloved home. His unbelieving eyes could hardly comprehend as many of his buildings went up in flames or were ruthlessly vandalized. After the war, he and his "family" tried to pick up the pieces and gather in the children once more. But with the declaration of independence in 1949, he felt it best to deed the home to the Javanese Church. Today the children still sleep in temporary bamboo dorms, many of which they have constructed by themselves. In late 1952, Dr. Clarke received an urgent request from Superintendent Probowinoto, "Please help my children, if you can." American sponsors responded with alacrity and many of the nut-brown youngsters were soon "adopted."

Another difficulty faced by Christians, particularly in West Java, is the predominance of Islamic groups, as well as the damage done in World War II. Growing out of this situation, Tandjong Barat Orphanage in the capital city of Djakarta was one of the first spontaneous activities of the Javanese Church. Many of the Christian villages were irreparably devastated by the bombings of the War. Fleeing the flames and shrapnel, hundreds of parents and children died of wounds, exhaustion or starvation. One child, a four-year-old, was picked up with streaming head wounds and brought to a Javanese chapel. The parents had been found, dead, beside her. Others were found wandering along the muddy roadside, while still others lay in the muck too weak to move. The little church, struggling in the midst of a hostile religion, managed somehow to scrape enough money together to secure a building and some ground near Djakarta.

It was with scraps from the tables and left-over rags that the children were fed and clothed at first. Resources were meagre everywhere at the time, and the ever-growing family of orphans lived precariously through the postwar and post-independence years. "Many times," related Mr. Suramin Dantji, "I was ready to close the doors. But then, God would answer our prayer and send us some food." In the mid-fifties, Mr. Suramin heard of CCF. An urgent request, "Please adopt my children," brought a welcome wire from Dr. Clarke, "Will 'adopt' all your children. Send their pictures and stories at once."

At the moment, all of Southeast Asia remains a great question-mark. President Kennedy, as did President Eisenhower before him, has requested billions to be poured into this crucial region. Most of these billions will be spent on armaments. The best investment dollar-for-dollar, however, will be the tangible love sent by Americans who "adopt" Asia's babies.

ELEVEN

Sad Song of India

SOME years ago, an Englishman described the poverty of India in these terms:

"Poverty is to see little children shrivel and die at the height of their beauty.

"I have seen children fighting over a meal of roasted rat. . .

"I have watched men climb trees to get red ants to eat instead of chillies.

"Poverty is hunger, frustration, bereavement, futility. There is nothing beautiful about it."

On January 26, 1950, ancient India, formerly part of the British Empire, was declared an independent Republic. But with Jawaharlal Nehru at its helm, the proud new nation had inherited the poverty and overpopulation of centuries, with the despair and anguish they bequeathed. Torn by an outmoded caste system, riven by inter-religious strife, disease-ridden and crowded, it struggled to rise to its feet. Five-year plans were declared to improve its economy. Birth-control plans were devised to stem its population growth. Castes were outlawed and schools were opened. But still the streets crawled with tired children and skeletal men.

Dr. Clarke entered the worst slum area in the whole subcontinent as early as 1948. There, in Calcutta, he talked to a

Methodist missionary named Walter Griffiths at the Lee Memorial Orphanage and arranged to help more children. Later, he said, "I remember that night when I left India. The purser had switched off all the plane's cabin lights. I reclined my seat, pulled my blanket about me, but I could not sleep. I was thinking about the poverty, the wretched poor in the streets. I was thinking, too, about the children I had met, talked to and held hands with in the Lee Memorial Mission of Calcutta. What beautiful and lovely children! How full of life and mystery and promise their shining black eyes! How bright they were and quick in answering my questions.

"Yet Dr. Griffiths, the superintendent, told me so many of them had been picked up in the streets of Calcutta and by the slightest of margins they had responded to the nursing and lived."

Founded in 1690 by England's "empire builder" Job Charnock, Calcutta has had a long and checkered career. Misery, poverty and death have dogged its footsteps. Seventy-five years ago, Rudyard Kipling found a Calcutta somewhat smaller (today's population is 4,000,000, making it India's largest metropolis) but otherwise almost identical to today's.

Death still looks down on Calcutta almost a century later. Periodically cholera epidemics wipe out thousands in this city hemmed in by the salt-marshes. In an area less than half the size of the District of Columbia, there are 135,000 people living to every square mile. They cluster on the streets, where families mark off a patch on the sidewalk as "theirs."

A traveller described how he saw a baby struggling to drink milk from the shrunken breast of his dead mother. Beggars swarm the thoroughfares on stumps of legs or hold out stumps of arms. The noise and jangle of horns, whistles, bells and loud cries assault the air day and night.

Children are conceived, born, exist and die on the teeming sidewalks. Every day 300 of them are born. In famine times the municipality collects dead bodies from the curbs, for every night hundreds go to sleep never to awaken again.

Recently the refugees have been removed from the Sealdah Railroad Station where for years 4,000 ate, slept, cooked, quarreled, made love. They napped on the platforms, around the ticket windows, under the benches.

Little wonder that one-fifth of the city's people follow Communism's will-o-the-wisp. The sparkling promises seem to light their future where there is so little hope. In 1955 when Khrushchev and Bulganin visited Calcutta, the Reds were able to muster 2,000,000 people in the streets to scream hysterical cheers.

It has been Dr. Clarke's dream since 1948 that CCF can help lead the way in India in showing the true concern and compassion inherent in Christianity. It is heartening to know that other Americans along with missionaries like the Griffiths have felt the same. The Central Government has made great strides with its five year program but India is vast and her problems gigantic.

In the heart of Calcutta, facing a lawn-green park, stands the three-story building of the Lee Memorial Orphanage. It seems much like a fairyland to children who are brought from the jammed streets or jumbled shacks where they had been abandoned.

The orphanage was founded many years ago by Methodist missionaries, Reverend and Mrs. David Hiram Lee. Assigned to a station on the slopes of the Himalayas near the border of Tibet, their compound had been built on a treacherous mountainside. During one of the annual rains, when both this missionary and his wife were preaching in the city of Darjeeling, their house was suddenly struck by a flash-flood and landslide. When they returned that afternoon, their splintered home was strewn down the slope. With grief in their hearts, they slowly retrieved the bodies of their six children.

Realizing the gravity of this blow, the Methodist Board furloughed the Lees to Calcutta, 300 miles to the south. As they slowly recuperated from their ordeal, the Lees began to notice the numbers of parentless children living in the squalor of the city streets. One day, David Lee returned to the mission compound with a scrawny baby in his arms. "I think it is going to die," he told his wife. "I found it in the gutter." For the next week, the Lees poured all the love and devotion formerly reserved for their six lost youngsters upon this tiny infant. It began to gain weight, to take an interest, to grow and to smile. Soon after that another toddler was brought to the mission home, this time by Mrs. Lee. Then there were six, then ten children, depending on the missionary and his wife.

Appealing to Methodist churches in America, the Lees soon received enough funds to buy their first dormitory in the very heart of Calcutta. The orphanage grew slowly, out of the desperate need of many children. The years passed and the Lees retired to America and died. Others took their place, however, and the Home continued to expand until it occupies a large portion of the city block on Raja Subodh Mullick Square. Hundreds of young victims of flood, war and famine have been welcomed into its shelter through the years. But as it grew its expenses became heavier, until finally in the late 1940's, Dr. Griffiths, the superintendent, appealed to Dr. Clarke and CCF for much-needed help. Today many CCF sponsors proudly write to "their" children at Lee Memorial.

On a 1956 trip, Dr. Clarke described what he saw there: "I wish you could have seen it all when I visited them. There is a separate building where all the meals are prepared," he said, and then added, "I must tell you—the girls do all the cooking themselves! There is a little hospital, too, and a bath house off one end of the roomy court, which serves as a playground for the little ones, as well as a place for exercise and sports for the older children.

"The schoolrooms were very much like our own, with their desks and books and blackboards. The sleeping quarters were very different, however. 'This is where the children sleep,' Reverend Griffiths explained as he showed me through the third-floor dormitories. 'But where?' I started to ask, as I looked at the barren rooms. And then I saw the neat rolls of bedding around the walls. Indian fashion, these would be unrolled at night and the little sleepers would rest and dream quite as well on the floor as we do in our downy beds at home.

"They all looked sweet and smiling and happy as Superintendent Griffiths took me about to inspect them at school and work and play. 'These children are all good students,' he said proudly, as we made our way from the kindergarten through the grades and the Teachers' Training classes. In addition to their studies, the girls must learn handwork, sewing, cooking and housekeeping. The boys learn gardening, carpentry and various handcrafts. Older girls often take nurses' training in the Methodist mission hospital while others head for college courses."

The proudest part of his report, Dr. Clarke saved for the last. "I think maybe," he said, "you would like me to tell you about the results these courses have produced. Some of our older boys, upon graduating, have immediately secured positions as welders in large factories, motor mechanics in local garages and assembly plants, sheet metal-workers with plumbing contractors, and electrical workers with Calcutta radio and TV repair shops. Virtually all the girls become teachers; a few become nurses. All of them are children in whom we take pride. I know you are pleased, too, to know that our children are thus doing their share in helping their country in its economic awakening."

In 1960, Verent Mills visited Lee Memorial and there he

found a touching sight—Helen Lee, a bedridden patient who was celebrating her birthday. She has suffered from rheumatoid arthritis for five years. Some of the other girls had braided her hair with pink ribbons for her party, for her cheery smile has made her the most popular youngster in the orphanage. Dr. Griffiths told Mills that Helen's body is now almost rigid. She is able to move only one limb—her left arm, about six inches. Her lower jaw moves only a quarter of an inch and all her food must be mashed and forced between her teeth. But she keeps smiling and lightens the entire Home.

Mrs. Griffiths, the superintendent's wife, told Verent Mills a bit more about this lovely girl and another youngster in the Home: "A little over two years ago, a little orphan girl named Barati came to Lee Memorial and asked to be taken in. Her mother and father had been teachers in Calcutta but were killed in the Moslem-Hindu clashes around 1950. Barati was then taken into a neighbor's home as a slave girl. Soon the neighbor left for another part of India but, before leaving, sold Barati to another family.

"Finally, Barati came to our door. 'I hear,' she said, 'that you teach little girls how to sew. Could you teach me so I could earn a living? I couldn't learn much else because I guess I am too old to go to school.'

"I went to the home where Barati was living," said Mrs. Griffiths, "and made arrangements for her to come to Lee Memorial. After she had been with us for only a few days, I discovered that the youngster was unusually intelligent. I took her to Helen's bedside and introduced them. A warm friendship soon developed and our 'paralyzed angel' offered to tutor Barati. Every day after that I would find Barati sitting beside Helen's bed from early morning to late at night—learning to read and write.

"At the end of four months," Mrs. Griffiths went on, "although it seems almost unbelievable, Barati had completed

reading all the schoolbooks up through the sixth grade. She
had actually mastered the reading, writing, spelling and arith-
metic and was ready to enter the next grade. So at the beginning of the next semester, we put her in with her own age
group. This year she has been in the top 25 per cent of her
class. And," added Mrs. Griffiths, "Helen is so proud!"

Perhaps this is the place to add two more names of "un-ugly
Americans" to the long list of thousands who labor around
the world bringing the message of freedom, truth and love.
Dr. and Mrs. W. G. Griffiths have ministered in Calcutta for
over forty years as Methodist missionaries. Dr. Clarke credits
them as the "true heart" of the orphanage in these words:
"Most of all it is Reverend and Mrs. Griffiths who make this
a truly happy home. This kindly couple has been as devoted
to their little Bengalese boys and girls as any real mother and
father could. No wonder the children love them so!"

In the late fifties, Christian Children's Fund was to play
a minor but significant role in the action against Communist
encroachment in Kerala State, South India. There, at the
CCF-owned Alwaye Settlement, the firm policy of non-violent
opposition helped the cause of Christianity and freedom.

During India's second general election in February and
March of 1957, the control of Nehru's Congress Party remained secure. Only in one state, Kerala, did the Communists
gain the ascendancy. There, in characteristic fashion, the Reds
set to work to undermine the labors of the Christian church.
The National Government had in 1958 passed a resolution
charging Kerala with insecurity, discrimination and murderous
assaults on non-Communists. Undaunted, however, the Communist regime in the state passed an education bill author-
izing government control of all schools receiving any state-aid.
The bill was rightly interpreted as an attack on Christian
schools which constitute a majority of the educational institutions in Kerala.

However, other forces were working against them. On March 17, 1959, the Dalai Lama, escaping the Communist Chinese oppression in Tibet, crossed the border and was admitted by the Indian Government into Mussoorie, Uttar Pradesh. Angered, the Red Chinese accused India of complicity in the Tibetan "resistance." Rapidly Indian popular opinion turned against China in almost every important center. On August 28th, Chinese troop detachments occupied portions of India's North-East Frontier. On October 21st, in the area of Ladakh, a Chinese ambush killed nine members of an Indian patrol and captured seven others. Outraged public spokesmen demanded a strong stand against this obvious aggression.

It was in the heat of this climate of public anger that Dr. Clarke wired William Henry, then CCF's superintendent at Alwaye, to withstand Communist confiscation by every legal means. The Christian communities stood firm and by late '59, the tide had turned against the Communists in Kerala. The State assembly was dissolved and new elections were demanded. The Red opposition had overplayed its hand.

Founded at the turn of the century by English missionaries, Alwaye Settlement has proved to be one of the noblest undertakings in India. A Christian young man studying in that part of India one day found a hungry orphan on the road. He had been driven from the nearby village because he was an outcaste. Temporarily taking the child in, he soon discovered that many other outcaste youngsters were wandering the streets, ostracized from the community by Hinduism's ancient rules. With two other students, the young missionary built the first dormitory of Alwaye Settlement. Then a school was erected for the unhappy children—there were more of them by now. Twenty years passed and the little orphanage and school had grown into a big one. It had its own chapel, workshop, farm, dairy and orchard. It also had built a Community

Center which served not only its own needs—but the social needs of the entire countryside.

Then just as it had reached a peak of usefulness, Hitler's Panzer divisions rolled into Poland. England, with her back to the wall, could no longer send missionary support. Weeds began to grow in the fine fields at Alwaye and jackals came to live in the bush. The children were left without adequate care and many drifted away. Alwaye became almost a deserted village. The cattle dwindled; the trees went without pruning; the walls of the houses crumbled—then a great famine struck South India and hundreds more children were left homeless.

At this time, a friend wrote Dr. Clarke, "Children and orphanage lands are going to waste in South India. Investigate Alwaye!" Investigate he did and quickly took the Settlement over. Within a short time he had dispatched Reverend and Mrs. Clare Scratch and their family to supervise its rehabilitation. Within eight months it was transformed. The hills that comprise much of the farm had been cleared and were beautifully terraced. Terraces were even shored up with blocks of laterite that had been dug from the ground. Old trees were reclaimed and new trees were planted—cashew, mango, jackfruit and papaya. And along side those, banana, date and coconut palm.

With the help of the State Department of Agriculture and CCF's agricultural expert, the best varieties of pineapple and pepper vines were selected and planted up and down the terraces. A strain of rice, developed by the Settlement's Mr. George was acknowledged by the government and named "Settlement Paddy" in honor of Alwaye. Sugar cane was soon waving its fronds in the fields. Beehives are carefully tended daily. Lemon grass provides a supply of oil of citronella for public sale.

At the foot of the big hill is the barn where Alwaye's young people are experimenting with cross-bred cattle which it is hoped will better stand the climate of the area. The Settlement's cows produce three times as much milk as India's average.

Down the hill from the church is the school, and below that on a gently sloping grade, is the clinic where the children bring their cuts and bruises. Then comes the Industrial School where the boys make their own textiles and hammer out beautiful furniture.

In a 1958 visit to Alwaye, Dr. Clarke met one of the hundreds of children who have been brought to the Settlement. His heart was so touched by this tiny youngster that when he returned to the States he presented her peculiar need to Americans in these words: "Nothing was known about Unbu. In India names have a meaning and her name means 'love' but she has never had any. She was found in a small village on the plains of South India, in the early morning. She had a coconut shell which she was using to beg with. She was sobbing and no one knew how she came to the village. She had evidently been dropped there deliberately by someone during the night. She had not been there the day before.

"She explained the long gash in the side of her head by saying that she was torn by the claws of a dog. The animal had knocked her down to take the few scraps of food someone had put in her coconut shell. She shook her head when asked about her mother and father and said she never had any.

"She did not know the place where she came from. She just knew that it 'was big.' She seemed to think she had always been in the streets alone. She had never eaten a regular meal, merely scraps put in her shell. Sometimes she had a few grains of rice or some vegetables she bought for a few annas (an anna is worth about two United States pennies) when she was lucky enough to be given any. She had never been in a house. She always slept on the streets. Her stomach always hurt."

When Unbu's story was published, hundreds of Americans again responded from every state in the Union. Their gifts and good wishes came in like a flood. Now she has been "adopted" and plays happily with other children in the Home in India.

This is the story of millions in India today. In a population of 400,000,000, and with a birth-rate of 40 to every 1,000 people, the nation represents one of the most sorely pressed in the world. It is reliably estimated that 30 per cent of India's people suffer from continual hunger. At least a million die every year from malaria while a half million succumb to tuberculosis. At least the same number perish from smallpox. Plagues of cholera and dysentery ravage whole areas each year in which people die by the thousands. The number of physicians is woefully inadequate and there is only one hospital to every 105,000 persons. Although great strides have been made in education, 70 per cent of the population can still neither read nor write.

Under Dr. Clarke's guidance, CCF turned its attention to this area in 1948 for the first time. Since then the number of Homes helped in India has increased to twenty-three, and the number of children to 2,500. And there are a great number of homes on the waiting list, having petitioned for CCF assistance.

TWELVE

Hunger by the Taj Mahal

OVER the decade of the fifties, CCF's work continued to expand in India. Letters of appeal poured into Dr. Clarke's office from every quarter of that great country. Many of them had a tremendous urgency. The following was just one of scores:

"There are two things especially I hate to mention because I know how hard pressed you are on every hand. First, because of the desperate state here with children so needing our help, can we take in more children? For example, a girl was brought in recently who was found under a bench in a third-class train compartment. She is only four and could not answer our questions. I admit we took her in. If we had not, besides her hunger, she probably would have become prey of some evil person who would mistreat her and form bad habits for her. We have room for twenty more who are in equally desperate, pitiful need. We are their only hope."

Dr. Clarke's heart touched, he replied to this particular letter in these words, "CCF will help. Do not leave the children in loneliness and hunger. We will try to raise the money for their care."

The case-histories of the children came in by the hundreds.

138

Each told a different story of tragedy, but each had the same ending—misery for another child.

Case 166 reads: "This little girl's father died just before she was born. This tragedy so deranged the mother that after Ammini's death she wandered off leaving the baby alone. A neighbor took pity but was so desperately poor he had no food to spare. She was finally brought to us—skin and bones."

Case 167 was little better: "Nothing whatever is known of the home or parents of this little girl," it read. "She was picked up along the roadside, in pathetic condition, by a kindly missionary when she was a baby. The missionary placed her in an orphanage where she has lived for the past four years. For lack of funds, however, that home had to let Mariama, among others, go. Thereupon she was sent to us."

Case 182 told the story of Mary: "Her father was killed in a dynamite blast leaving the mother and four little girls without support. The mother went to work in the fields but her earnings were so meagre that she never could buy enough rice. She slowly starved herself to death so that her children could have bare sustenance. Then the children were brought to us— thin and naked—and we could not turn them away."

Redoubling his efforts during the decade of the 1950's, Dr. Clarke added orphanages to the CCF list as funds permitted. In some cases, too, he was able to authorize more dormitories for existing orphanages so that additional children could be taken in.

Throughout the fifties waves of famine swept across India. Hungry, gaunt people dragged their skeleton-bodies across vast stretches in search of a few grains of rice. "In many villages," said the missionaries, "we heard the groaning rise in the hot still air. The shrill cries of hollow children rent the stillness. They did not cry for rice itself, just for *fan*—water from the boiled rice. They knew the other was not to be had."

"In the highways," said another, "I beheld the parched skin

of beggars stretched over their clearly-visible skeletons. They muttered for 'rice' until they lapsed into coma—and death. The odor of the decaying bodies could be smelled for miles."

Children fought like wild animals for the privilege of scraping fetid garbage pails. Dogs, gone wild with hunger, shriveled and perished in the hot sun. Outside Jubbalpore on the banks of the Narbado, a tiny child huddled next to a shack. The hot sunlight beat down on his naked form. He slowly rocked his head in his hands. He was nauseous from hunger. "Mother," he suddenly cried, "I am dying. Let me drink some *fan* before I go."

One CCF staff member told Dr. Clarke of a tragic scene he had beheld near the village of Wadi: "As I trudged along the bank of the River Bhima," he said, "I saw a group of youngsters under a banana tree. Their arms and legs were mere sticks—their ribs stood out like cages under their skin. Gathered around a woman stretched on the ground, they watched with sad eyes as she gasped for breath. I soon discovered she was their mother. A mask of tragedy was on each little face as she breathed her last."

It was just such problems as these that had always touched the hearts of Christian workers. Wanting to do what they could to alleviate such suffering, they had founded hospitals, schools, churches, orphanages. In late 1953 a woman missionary named Mrs. Johnson Edwards was confronted by sights that demanded her action. Gathering hungry children around her skirts, she too started a Home. Later, describing the founding of her work, she said, "I started the orphanage in a small rented building in Madras. I had to do something for I saw the native children picking up food from garbage cans, often sharing the lean pickings with stray dogs. The hot sun here soon spoils food, but the children and the dogs were so hungry they ate it.

"My children whom I have picked up," she continued,

"were always so pitiful in their hunger. For example, recently three children were brought to me, two girls and a baby boy of 18 months. Their father was an auto driver who was killed in an accident. Their mother was a sickly woman and there was nothing to eat in the house. One day when the baby boy cried too long from hunger, she hanged herself. Neighbors hearing the wailing of the children came in and discovered the mother's body. They brought the youngsters to me. The baby boy we could not nurse back to health—he was too far gone. He died three days later, but the two girls are still with us—lovable and as sweet as any two youngsters can be."

Mrs. Edwards called the Home, Mrs. Webb's Memorial Orphanage, in honor of the lady who bought the first building. The quarters are now large enough to accommodate 275 children. Within the compound are a separate kitchen building and a small building for storage, as well. Nearby is a little space for a playground, and next to it a patch that is devoted to the growing of vegetables. The children are still quite cramped for Mrs. Edwards' cannot say "no" to any hungry child who knocks on her gate. But they are happy because they have her love and the love of the many Americans who have "adopted" them.

CCF staff members continued its work in many parts of India during the decade of the 1950's helping the many needy orphanages that required aid. One CCF worker dispatched to India by Dr. Clarke saw sights so unbelievable that he wrote the following to headquarters in Richmond:

"It couldn't be real, I thought it must be an optical illusion caused by the heat. It just didn't seem possible. The beggar boy drew nearer to me. I soon saw it was real enough. He was filthy, of course, with the specially nauseating filth found in Indian waifs. His hair was matted, alive with vermin. His arms, feet and chest festered with sores. He could not have washed for months. His eyes held that glazed, out-of-focus look common to beggar children in the middle and Far East who have been subjected to doping.

"But it was his face that struck horror in me. The skin of his forehead was drawn tightly together at the center. A sharp, strong little piece of wood was forced through horizontally. Descending from the middle of this was a longer piece—whose pointed end drove through his tongue which protruded from his mouth. His nose had been slightly flattened in the process. The tongue wound, though old, hadn't healed—it couldn't possibly heal that way—and was swollen, pus-filled. When the boy stood still, flies buzzed around and into his permanently opened mouth.

"Someone had obviously gone a little further than the usual methods employed by some poor Indian families in mutilating a child so that he would be more 'appealing' when he begged.

"My first reaction, after a close-up, was as much wonder as shock. How did he eat? How could he stay alive?

"We made a brief wayside stop here for a sip out of our cool water-flasks and a sandwich. But after this sight, the water and bread almost rose up inside me. We stopped in the next town to report what I had seen to the local authorities. The police inspector listened politely and then told me there was nothing he could do. 'Can you direct me to a physician, then?' I asked. He shook his head. There was none within fifty miles."

This was an extreme case to dramatize a beggar-child, it is true. But it is also true that the condition of over 90 per cent of the children in India is pitiful. Seven families out of ten live in grinding poverty. In most homes the total monthly income is Rs. 15-20 (between $3.20 and $4.20).

Thousands of children roamed the land uncared for during the fifties.

They still do during the sixties. Some have never known any parents. Most orphans are ill-treated and many are cruelly exploited. Girls are sold for temple service as prostitutes, although the authorities are trying to keep a closer check on this. Infant and child mortality is incredibly high.

One of the things that so often strikes the tourist in India as, indeed, in the whole Far East, is the perfunctory way children are exploited for sex. In Calcutta, solicitors accost tourists on every street, although it is illegal to do so. But there are so few police. Here a young Moslem offers the body of a ten-year-old girl. Over there, homosexuality is offered— an eight-year-old boy. The children have been taught to go through the motions of seduction. They do it mechanically. They do it for a crust of bread, a few grains of rice. They are victims of a famine too immense for them to comprehend, far more greatly sinned against than sinning.

Another of the problems that race and caste discrimination has brought upon India is the plight of orphan children with mixed-blood. Their distress is often worse than that of the outcastes, say some. "At least the outcastes have their own people," they argue. A few special orphanages have been founded just to care for these pitiful tots. One of these, Dr. Graham's Home is located at Kalimpong in West Bengal. There, 5,000 feet above the sea, in the cool clean air of the Himalayas, on the very road that leads to Mount Everest and Tibet a Presbyterian missionary had founded a Home at the turn of the century. Gathering these children whose origins stemmed from both East and West, he began to bring them into his own house. When he first founded his community, "on a shoestring," he had six youngsters and two staff members.

Dr. Graham had been appalled at the neglect of these children. "They are our own flesh and blood," he told the British. "We must do something about them." The next step was a small cottage in which to put his little "family"—they were the first six who had come to him with pleading eyes. Soon the interest of other Westerners was enlisted. Queen Mary herself was among those who showed a lively interest in the home. Before long the little hill ponies with their melodious bells were climbing the steep ascent from the tiger-infested Teesta Valley. On their backs they bore small, fair burdens with a hint of Eastern features. Up the road also came stout-hearted women from Dr. Graham's native Scotland, ready to teach and "mother" these youngsters. This was the beginning of a unique city of children, built on the roof of the world.

Today, there is a magnificent collection of seventy solid buildings of varying sizes sprawling over 500 acres. Caring for the 550 boys and girls are a capable group of men and women. There is a hospital with sixty beds that has a European doctor and trained nurses in charge. Food is supervised by a dietitian. The farm produces all the vegetables required. There are cows, pigs, chickens, horses. The staff of seventy includes House Mothers who are specialists in the "cottage system." The curriculum in the school, besides regular primary and secondary training, provides girls with a nurses' training course. The boys are trained in small handcrafts.

Founded originally for Anglo-Indians, the Home is now shared with their full-blooded Indian brothers and sisters. Two youngsters, a boy and a girl, were brought recently. Their father, a police officer in the Bengal Service, had come home one night and shot his wife dead. Then he turned the revolver on himself and took his own life. It was discovered that he had been a sexual deviate. The children's grandmother suffered such mental shock that she was certified for the local asylum. The boy, aged eight, and his ten-year-old sister were badly shaken by the double killing and needed special therapy for months. They were brought to the Dr. Graham's Home by their grandfather, too aged, poor, and infirm to watch over them. Only the care and love shown at the Orphanage has removed from their young faces the traces of the tragedy. The

American "parents" who have "adopted" them through CCF are delighted with their progress and their happy letters.

Other CCF staff workers reporting from widely separated areas in India sent case-histories on other children that needed care. There were not accommodations yet available for them, but Dr. Clarke went to work immediately to provide bed and board so that they might be cared for. One staff member reported an experience in Madras:

"I waited at the curb for a traffic light yesterday, when I felt something touch my shoe. I looked down. A hunger-racked face peered up at me. It surmounted a distended stomach, an unbelievably thin chest, a neck about the thickness of the upper part of a baseball bat and limbs comparable in girth to the handle of a tennis racket. The child—it seemed to be a boy somewhere between eight and thirteen years of age—had prostrated himself at my feet and, as I bent down, he once more touched my shoe with his forehead.

"I asked through one of our party: 'Have you no one to look after you?' He shook his head, tapped his stomach, then held out his hand again in supplication. We gave him some coins. I asked him a little about his history.

"He told me his father had starved to death before the partition of Bengal. His mother died of exhaustion and exposure in the terrible trek out of East Pakistan which the family, like thousands of other Hindus, made after Independence. A relative gave him 'shelter'—four feet of sleeping space beneath a bunk. Everything he begged went to this man. Any day he went 'home' with less than a rupe (21 cents) he didn't get enough to eat; sometimes he didn't eat at all."

Dr. Clarke, in writing to sponsors in the autumn of 1955, reported: "Unhappy India has just suffered one of the worst floods in her history. Unceasing floods in India and Pakistan have wrecked more than 28,000 villages, damaged or destroyed the homes of 45,000,000 persons!" Trouble seems never to cease. Almost every month there comes an additional appeal to CCF's headquarters from orphanages and children in India—"Please help us!" Dr. Clarke has often stated, "If all the money that CCF raises annually—in the neighborhood of four to five million dollars—were to be concentrated on the needs of India's children, it would barely scratch the surface of the need there. India, with its 400,000,000 people, is still the land of the most poverty on earth, of hunger and suffering."

Yet all is not darkness there. The Government is laboring heroically to bring that dark land up toward the sun. Likewise, thousands of missionaries and hundreds of thousands of Americans are sending their aid, their prayers, their love to the little children.

In a 1958 visit to India, Dr. Clarke spoke of one other thing—"The people often share, even out of their desperate poverty. In Calcutta I saw a beggar take a coin from his own cup and put into another man's. What little he had he shared, for the other beggar was even worse off. He was blind."

Now assisting or completely supporting twenty-three orphanages and 2,500 children, CCF is planning considerable expansion in the near future. Mr. Deben Das, Secretary of the Food and Relief Committee in Calcutta wrote in early 1960, "There are still many areas in need. Thousands are starving, especially in the East Bengal area. The food crisis now is much more grave and distressing than in the famine of 1953."

How much the help of Dr. Clarke and his un-ugly Americans means is exemplified in a report recently received from the Government on St. George's School—a CCF-affiliate—in Madras: "I am very much impressed with what I saw there. The chairman of the School said, 'If it were not for CCF, we would have to close up.' Now they are not only still operating, but they are one of the best schools in the district. So often we hear the same story, 'CCF has saved the day!'"

THIRTEEN

Westward to the Near East

By 1950, the cry of children from another quarter reached the ears of CCF's International Director. This time it was from an area long familiar to him—the Near East.

Ever since the terrible massacres of Armenians in the early part of the twentieth century, the pitiful survivors had been wanderers on the face of the earth. Ousted from their native Armenia, which is now a part of Soviet Russia, they had clustered in other countries. Some had fled to Persia (Iran), others to Syria, and still others to Jordan and Lebanon. A few had crossed over into Greece and a number had remained in Turkey. Retracing steps he had taken long years before when he worked for Near East Relief, Dr. Clarke found heartache and misery. Writing of a visit there in the early fifties, he said:

"Fifty-five per cent of Jordan's total population are refugees. Many of these, of course, are from the 1948 Palestinian War when over a million Arabs were displaced. Syria, Lebanon, and the Gaza Strip also have been crowded with these pathetic folk. Especially cruel and hard is the lot of the Arab and Armenian refugees living in tents and in slums of cities like Beirut and Damascus.

"It is difficult to describe the misery of these slums, those

147

rickety old shacks made of rusted tin, worm-eaten boards and rubble from destroyed buildings. They give but little shelter from the hot semi-tropical sun or the relentless rain that makes mud of their dirt floors and soaks the old rags they sleep on. I cannot drive from my mind the listless children, either."

By the middle of 1955 he was able to write, "CCF has more than doubled its work in these three countries but I would give anything if I could do more. These poor little neglected children put a lump in my throat and an ache in my heart.

"When I think what a little money can do for these children! It can take off their dusty rags, heal the sores on their thin bodies, give them milk to drink and a warm stew with some meat in it.

"It could wash the beautiful black hair of a little orphan girl who smiled at me during one of my inspection trips. How she would have loved a ribbon for her hair! Her whole life could be changed. To take her away from those drab and horrible shacks, away from the filth and smell and let her know of God's love—what a lot could be done. But none of this happened for her. She is still there. There was no money for me to place her in an orphanage. Did CCF fail her?"

The refugees were still there in 1961. Many had had forty years of wandering. One family visited by Dr. Clarke in Lakia, Syria was living in a dilapidated mud-brick hut. There were three generations dwelling there. One of them was a lad who had lost both arms and legs in the bitter war of 1948. He was propped in the corner on a vermin-infested rush mat.

In Lebanon he saw the hovels that accommodated 100,000 refugees. He saw some of the babies that were born there. Each new baby was labelled by the Lebanese Government as "Palestinian."

Around Damascus, Syria, he saw the vast slums that held 45,000 more of these hapless, hopeless people. Members of his staff also brought him word of the "no man's land" in the Gaza Strip. There is a tiny twenty-five-mile stretch of land that reaches from Rafa on the Egyptian border to a mile or so north of Gaza, where 250,000 refugees have been crammed.

There were 1,000,000 others beside the Armenians—innocent pawns of international bickering. The Arab nations insisted on the re-establishment of the 1947 frontiers that existed before the Palestinian War. They also insisted on the return of these 1,000,000 refugees to their original homes plus a financial compensation. The Israel Government was equally adamant that such responsibility be shared proportionately by all the nations involved. It was a deadlock that promised little for the future. Meanwhile, the children suffer.

Into one of the world's most forsaken areas, near Lebanon's Valley of Bekaa, 3,000 Armenians had been forced to flee. "It is so desolate," wrote Mrs. Clarke, "that one wonders how man or beast can manage to survive." Here on a barren, stony strip of land at the village of Aindjar, a settlement was provided by the government. Funds were only sufficient, however, for the building of cheerless, windowless cement block huts, twelve by fourteen. There, between two hills in the Anti-Lebanon Mountains, these folk huddled and existed. The occupants slept and ate on the hard mud floors. Their only heat in winter was a rare fire built in the middle of the hut with scanty branches of thorn bush, the only native vegetation in the area. Despite a climate that brought blinding heat in the summer, the winters were bitter cold, often burying the drab village in three feet of snow. During the summer period, the temperature often reached 110 degrees. The flat concrete huts were poor protection from the blazing sun. In these one-room dwellings, the young were born and the old died. Here, too, the animals were housed and meagre supplies were stored.

On the verge of starvation in the middle fifties, these desperate people turned to CCF for aid. Soon "adoptions" of helpless children there were arranged.

Two kindly Lutheran sisters were appointed by CCF as superintendents of a special type of Home. They had come originally with their few school books, their medicine kits, and their hearts filled with compassion—Sister Hedwig Aenishanslin from Switzerland, and Sister Maria Rock from Germany. They had set up a clinic, opened a school, and conducted church services. But their facilities were extremely limited. They used some old broken-down shacks for classrooms, clinic and chapel. Then CCF stepped in to feed the children properly and to improve the classrooms. Soon adequate nourishment was reflected in a bright new alertness among the boys and girls. Extensions were built on the existing buildings and new benches and tables were added. Older children who had never had the opportunity to learn were taught to read and write. The girls learned to knit and sew. The boys learned how to make toys, to do tailoring, to cultivate a garden. In fact, under CCF's tutelage, their trees, shrubs and flowers have literally made the desert bloom like the rose.

Finally, in 1956 CCF built a brand-new school—modern, bright, airy and colorful. It lifted the morale of the whole settlement with its warm dry floors, its blackboards, lockers, desks and cement walks.

Life began to stir at Aindjar. The girls formed a Girls' Association that met weekly. The women met in the new school building every Wednesday night for sewing lessons. The children learned how to play. Sister Maria wrote to Mrs. Clarke, "They knew absolutely nothing about playing. What joy they got from the little games of our own native places!"

Clothing improved, too. At first, few had a change of clothing. On Saturday everyone had to "disappear" while their clothes were being washed. Soon shipments of new clothing were on the way from CCF sponsors in America. A new chapel was erected, too. And, the greatest wonder of all, a mysterious crate arrived from Switzerland soon after: Eagerly pried open by the older boys it proved to be—a bell for the steeple!

In describing this area of the world to me recently, CCF's Coordinator, Reverend Verent Mills said, "I think the most tragic youngsters in the Near and Middle East are the blind children. There are so many in proportion to the total population! Perhaps it is due to the many dust storms as well as the bad sanitation and malnutrition."

These sightless tots come from families so destitute in many cases that they live in culverts under the streets. Because food is so limited there is never enough for a little blind child. Many of them come from homes high in the mountains where a sightless child is considered a burden. Others come from parents who have cast them out on the dusty streets and never want to see them again. It is for children such as these that the CCF affiliated Homes for Blind Girls and Boys were founded in Bethlehem, Jordan. Here, for the first time in their lives, the children discover that they are loved.

One of the very interesting things about these homes is that its superintendent, Miss Adele Dafesh, is herself blind, as are a number of her teachers. Far from being a handicap, her blindness has proven an asset time and time again. It has given her a sympathy and understanding that a sighted teacher could learn only after many years. Having herself gone through many years of study in a darkened world, *she knows.*

Most of the three-score children in her care, ranging in age from four to fourteen years, come to her from the street. The most familiar lines in their case-histories are: "There is little information on the parents of this child. They are probably dead—but the circumstances are unknown." Frequently, too, the last line of the report reads, "This child was born blind."

CCF workers reported to Dr. Clarke in 1956 that there were hundreds of Arab and Armenian orphan boys and girls wandering in the camps throughout Gaza, as well as in Lebanon, Jordan and Syria. One emaciated lad put out his hand to the traveller with the words, "I am a refugee boy. Help me and Allah will bless you!"

To meet the needs of children like this, St. Margaret's Home-School was established in Nazareth. The Palestinian War of 1948 caused the death of so many parents that St. Margaret's was transformed from a day school into an orphanage. Originally run entirely by the Church of England, this turn of affairs brought the institution serious financial reverses. The sources of funds in England could not meet the new requirements, and the superintendent wrote Dr. Clarke asking for CCF assistance.

The girls who now live at St. Margaret's have straggled in from the vast refugee camps in Israel. Ragged and forlorn, they have been unwanted everywhere, rejected by the towns and villages where their parents once lived and died. These towns and villages are composed of stones, pieces of tin, rubble, dried mud. The men and women living there "temporarily" for thirteen years have grown resentful and bitter. "We have a past," they say, "but no future." Many of them have given up hope of anything but the dreary, dirty, wretched shacks in which they live. They have grown to hate themselves and their neighbors, to whom they barely speak. Most of them sit and stare vacantly. "The future is death," say many. As for the orphan children who cluster around the outskirts, hoping for a crust of bread, they have nothing for them—not even a curse.

Here in the village where Jesus lived as a boy, this orphanage gives the love that He would give. Five small buildings compose the Home. There is a large garden where the girls play. The Home raises its own lettuce, spinach, olives, figs, plums, apricots and lemons. The youngsters have their own school here, their own dolls, their own games. They are also taught to sew, cook and keep house. Every morning and every evening they learn anew the meaning of prayer to a heavenly Father whose Son lived nearby many years ago.

Dr. Clarke has visited and re-visited in these countries in recent years. Always his report was the same, "It made my heart sick to look at the children, at their rags, at their homes, at their pinched faces."

"A little girl came toward me, hesitantly," he reported after a 1959 trip. "When her eyes looked into mine, I felt so unworthy. Jesus would have blessed her. But she passed me and went on into the darkness of one of the hovels—out of my life. It was almost as if I heard a voice saying, 'Inasmuch as ye have done it unto one of the least of these . . .' "

In another report, he stated, "Today, I saw three ragged children in Beirut. These wretched little ones were sitting beneath a wall on which a Communist slogan had been painted by a Red sympathizer. The slogan promised 'better things' through the Soviet way. Was this 'the handwriting on the wall,' in truth? How much longer can tourists from the West, from America, wine and dine in the best hotels in Beirut, oblivious to the pain and hunger of little boys and girls under their windows?"

Today, Christian Children's Fund assists such children in sixteen Homes and orphanages in the Near East. Every month support goes out to over 1,200 children from American sponsors to their "adoptees."

Letters to the children are often couched in terms of a very real affection. "Dear Loucine," reads one, "Daddy and Ruth and Mary send you their love. We were all so happy to get your nice card and letter. I was glad that the sweater fit you so well. Thank your teacher for me for sending the snapshot of you wearing it. It looks lovely on you. We are going to try and send you some picture books and a doll very soon. I hope you will like them. Write to us when you can. We all enjoy your letters so much. With all our love, Mother and Daddy Thompson, and Ruth and Mary."

One other of these Near Eastern Homes should perhaps be mentioned because of its unusual origin. It is called Badanegan Doun, or Boys' Home, and is located in Istanbul, Turkey. Here, a Christian pastor has taken boys from the streets of the city and has made a dormitory for them in the basement of his church. Many of these orphans—all of them are of Armenian origin—were footloose street urchins until Reverend Hrant Guzelian took them in and had barely managed to avoid starvation. They begged, ran errands, salvaged trash and ate half-rotten food from garbage pails. It was a hard life in which hunger dogged their young footsteps. At night they slept huddled in doorways and alleys. The luckier ones sometimes found a large pipe or culvert to sleep in. Many of them often sank from exhaustion on to the hard pavements or into a gutter.

Reverend Guzelian discovered one of them one morning searching through his garbage can. In a conversation that ensued, he found that this lad was just one of a group who lived under a tin shelter in his alley. Asking permission from his church, he found that his parishioners were equally anxious to help. Soon an "orphanage" had been established in the church's basement. The members worked hard to make it an attractive place for the boys by painting and scrubbing. Decent food was set before these lads at regular meal times, clean clothing was provided and cots were set up. They even collected a small library of books for the boys to read and study. Classes and worship services were conducted for them upstairs in the church auditorium. Games were organized for them in the courtyard behind the sanctuary.

Funds for food and clothing were limited, however. This was not a wealthy church. When Reverend Guzelian heard of CCF, therefore, he wrote a letter to Dr. Clarke explaining the needs. The work was of special interest to CCF's Director because he had labored so many years previously to help the parents and grandparents of these boys. Long past was the inhuman treatment of the Armenians by the Turks. Today, they live in amity and peace with their neighbors. Unfortunately, those who escaped from Armenia after World War I have existed in refugee camps all over the Near East ever since. Some have even fled to Greece where CCF helps two groups of them near Athens. The hapless Armenians have been wanderers on the face of the earth for two generations. These orphan boys touched Dr. Clarke's heart and CCF immediately sent aid. "Armenia," he said at the time, "as the oldest Christian nation on earth, deserves the concern of church people everywhere."

One of the boys at Badanegan Doun, deeply grateful to his sponsor, wrote,

"I had a good meal today. It is the first I have had since mother died three years ago. Thank you, dear sponsor, for sending me your help."

In his 1960 visit to Lebanon, Dr. Clarke spoke to a group of Armenian friends and, in passing, mentioned that he had visited there many years before as a director for Near East Relief. To his surprise, when he finished speaking, a distinguished looking man came up to him and bowed deeply. Taking Dr. Clarke's hand, he kissed it and then with tears trickling down his face said, "Ah, so you are my father. Many years ago I was one of those hundreds of Armenian children whose life you saved when you came to us in our distress." Today, this man, Reverend K. S. Tilkian, pastors the largest Armenian Church in Beirut. What gratification it was for CCF's Director to know that one of "his children" had risen from gutter to pulpit because of his youthful efforts!

In 1961, Dr. Clarke expressed to me his goal in the Near East in these words, "With one million Arab refugees in addition to our beloved Armenians, there are thousands more boys and girls who are asking our help. I hope we can give it."

Other calls of distress, however, were in his ears. They came from the "mother-countries" of most Americans—from Europe.

FOURTEEN

Europe's Children

On July 10, 1943, Allied forces landed in Sicily. From that day on, air bombardment of all Italian ports was intensified. The Ports of Genoa, Leghorn, Taranto and Naples suffered tragically. In the particular line of fire was the Portici section of Naples where Casa Materna Orphanage was located. The area was literally flattened and the casualties were appalling. Under such constant fire, the children had to be evacuated. When they returned after the Armistice of September 3rd, they discovered that the Home had been hit seven different times.

As were many of Naples' houses, the orphanage buildings had been shattered and looted. Much of the household equipment had been stolen or destroyed. But the youngsters immediately found that they had good friends in the English and American soldiers. These open-hearted soldiers brought food and money. They even took their boxing gloves and football leather to fashion little shoes for the children. On days off, they lent their muscles to restore the dormitories and classroom buildings. But the Home's financial needs continued in the postwar period until the superintendent, the venerable Riccardo Santi, wrote to Dr. Clarke. His letter reading,

157

"Please help," was answered by the succinct reply, "Help is on the way."

The Casa Materna Orphanage had been founded many years before when Reverend Riccardo Santi, a young Methodist minister, happened on two hungry and neglected looking children in the public square. "Where do you live?" he asked; "Everywhere," was their reply. Appalled by their condition and hopelessness, Pastor Santi took them home with him. That night he began to make inquiries, "Who takes care of homeless children?" The answer was discouraging. No one did.

At the next Sunday morning service, Pastor Santi shared his burden with the people of his parish. The good folk went home and soon returned. One brought a bed; another, a chair; some brought money; others brought clothing. The two tots were provided for in no time. It was not long, however, before other homeless children came to the parsonage door. Presently there were ten boys and girls—then fifty. Somehow, they got along. Friends helped them to locate a large apartment. The providence of God helped them pay the bills. Then a visiting commission, observing the fine work Pastor Santi was doing, bought them a home—a wonderful home. It had been the residence of the Prince of Monaco. The children felt transported to a fairyland for it was very beautiful with its seven acres of garden, its two large buildings and its beach, lying along the Bay of Naples.

Casa Materna soon gained the reputation of being one of the finest orphanages in Europe. Then World War II devastated its buildings! There was havoc on every hand. When the children returned to live in the shattered structures, there were hundreds of other orphans that needed care. In addition, Germany had declared war on its former ally and Nazi bombs were again shaking the home. The people of Naples and all southern Italy once more holed up in the caves. Eight thousand squashed into one hillside, ten thousand into another.

The populace looked out helplessly on the heaps of broken masonry that had once been their homes. Here and there in the smoke they saw blue sky framed in skeleton windows. The rescue teams' job was appalling. They would bring in the broken body of a child, and he would whisper that his parents were buried in the rubble.

The pitiful tots wandered the pock-marked streets of every Italian city. Some tottered along with glazed eyes. Others cried for their mothers. One youngster watched as laborers pulled down the teetering side of a building. Then he burst into silent tears. As the masonry fell to one side, a mass of dark curls dangled from the second floor. It was the lad's sister.

With each new bombardment, the children raced for shelter. They shrank from the earsplitting crash—the dazzling light—the concussive roar. Their terrified shrieks rent the air. In one courtyard, according to an Orphanage staff member, a tiny body was found clasping a dirty doll. She had not made the shelter in time.

Naples was crowded with children of every age. They were dressed in rags. Some wore tattered cast-offs from Allied uniforms. The G.I.'s found them in clusters or alone. Antonio, a dark-eyed boy of seven, was discovered in a Naples doorway, huddled back from the rain. The soldier put his arm around his thin shoulders and discovered he was wet and shivering. He opened a K-ration and watched as the lad gobbled it down. Searching for a good home, he eventually brought the youngster to Pastor Santi.

The staff workers at this CCF-affiliated Home, almost wept as they recalled the conditions of the children after V-E Day. For five years they roamed the streets, orphaned or deserted. They joined gangs or strayed hopelessly.

They lived in the rubble or in the caves. They were dirty, ragged, lice-covered. Most of them shook with cold or fever. "I saw one three-year-old," recalled a worker, "dressed in wrapping paper. It was held on him with wire." Another, a child of four, was naked. The month was January and he was crying bitterly.

There were so many of them. But the superintendent and his aides worked feverishly to take in all they could. They were still laboring against time five years later when CCF sponsors "adopted" their first children there. In 1954, Dr. Clarke reported to CCF friends, "There are many families in Naples still living in hovels made out of old tin cans, rusted iron and rubble. There is no running water or sanitary arrangements. Many badly nourished children wander about— too frequently they are orphans."

By that time, Christian Children's Fund was helping in two Italian orphanages. By 1961, the number of Italian Homes with CCF "adoptions" had increased to six, and the number of children to 500. By now, however, other areas in Europe had made known their desperation.

When the Iron Curtain clanged shut, untold suffering began for the innocent. Millions of dollars in property was confiscated as farms and villages were communized. Hundreds of thousands of people fled rather than lose their identity and their freedom. As the Russian troops moved across Eastern Germany, Czechoslovakia, Poland and other countries, untold brutalities were visited on the populace. A clergyman, reporting scenes he had witnessed in Upper Silesia, told of beatings, rape and murder. "The women, girls and children," he said, "suffered unspeakably." In his village, forty-one people lost their lives in resisting their "liberators," during a three-month period. Some of them the Russians had shot, some had been stabbed, some had been beaten to death or raped. Others had perished in fires deliberately set.

By the hundreds of thousands they fled across the border into West Germany. Dr. Clarke visited West Berlin in the early 1950's and watched as these pathetic folk straggled into freedom. A camp had been set up by the West German Government for the purpose of processing them. "The camp was a place of tragedy," Dr. Clarke remarked. "There were the family groups who had to desert the farms held by their ancestors for generations. They left behind their houses, barns, cattle, farm equipment, even the cats and dogs their children loved so. Some of the more fortunate families that I saw were intact. Many, however, had a father or children old enough to work in labor camps. Those had been picked up by the East German police. They have little hope of ever seeing them again."

Why were they fleeing? "Refugees are leaving East Germany in such large numbers because their farms were taken from them, or their places of business were confiscated by the Communist leaders. They leave, too, because of constant interference in their personal lives. There is perpetual uncertainty and fear, continued spying and mistrust."

One of the Homes in this area now aided by CCF is Rotthalmuenster Evangelisches Kinderheim, near the ancient city of Passau. Located on the border of Czechoslavakia and East Germany, the children here have seen much brutality and hatred. Passing by its doors almost daily is the influx of refugees escaping Soviet slavery. Nearby is the refugee camp of Schalding where many of the escapees have existed for years.

Originally, the Rotthalmuenster Kinderheim was located at Glatz in Upper Silesia. As the Russians invaded from the East and were within reach of the town, the superintendent hustled forty-five of his children on the last train. It was a bitter cold day and they saw the bodies of many youngsters as well as adults strewn along the tracks—frozen. It took this pathetic group four days of horror and anxiety to escape.

Eventually, they found safety in Passau, but their troubles were not over. After many days of suffering they found some damaged barracks near Rotthalmuenster that were connected with an old airfield. In time, funds were made available through sympathetic neighbors and the barracks were purchased. Crude repairs were made to keep out the bitter winds.

Deaconesses of the Lutheran Church soon came to mother these ragged children. Gradually the old buildings were improved with new roofs and alterations that added to their comfort. These kindly ladies have made a real home for the children who have seen such horror. Gifts and letters pour in every month from CCF sponsors in faraway America.

Karl Heinz, then aged eight, was typical of one of the earlier children "adopted" by an American sponsor. Karl's father, a farmer, was murdered in the fields by Russian soldiers. The boy and his mother lived precariously in their cottage for a few weeks afterward until Russian soldiers broke down the door. He still remembers the horror of watching as his mother was raped by these brutal men. When he tried to stop them with his puny strength, they knocked him unconscious with a blow. When he awoke they were gone and his mother with them. She never came back. Eventually, he wandered across the border into Rotthalmuenster and was found by a staff worker from the Home.

Children like Karl have been picked up by the hundreds as they wander along the border. In some of the twenty West German orphanages that CCF aids, as much as 60 per cent of the children are refugees from Communist tyranny. One thousand, five hundred helpless orphans in West Germany are now receiving love and training through the kindness of Americans who were once their "enemies."

To save still more of these waifs, CCF sponsors are now "adopting" Children at Braunschweig in what is perhaps the world's oldest orphanage. Approaching the Home, most visitors are startled to read the lettering over the doorway here: "Grosses Waisenhaus"—The Great Orphanage—Founded in 1245!" Two hundred and fifty years before Columbus discovered America, this venerable institution was saving children's lives. Now seven hundred years later it is still lifting tots by the hundreds out of turmoil and distress. Because of the financial troubles of the war from which it never has fully recovered the superintendent pleaded with CCF for assistance in the early fifties. Letters and gifts from sponsors to children have been flowing ever since.

Perhaps the most heart-rending of the recent refugees, however, have been the 200,000 that fled from Hungary in the fall and winter of 1956. All the world was galvanized as freedom-loving Hungarians rose on October 23rd to shake off the oppression of Russia. They fought with sticks and stones and bare fists. They fought with every weapon they could muster. Even their boys and girls of eleven and twelve fought. Against these pitiful odds, the Russian tanks roared through the streets of Budapest on November 11th to stage a "triumphant victory." Thirty thousand Hungarian patriots lay dead in the streets. Fifty thousand more were injured. There was a mass exodus of people who could not live in slavery.

Immediately, freedom-lovers everywhere gathered at the border to help these folk. Dr. Clarke dispatched CCF workers to watch for the many orphaned boys and girls and give them aid. There at Central Europe's Freedom Border, just inside Austria near the towns of Halbturn and Andau, camps were set up. Kindly Austrians lent their homes, their barns and other facilities.

"It was truly pitiful," read one report to Dr. Clarke. "All day long, every day during December and January, they trudged in. I heard children calling for their mothers. I saw dazed tots hugging dolls or teddy bears. I watched one sturdy little lad of eight—all alone—dressed in an oversized khaki jacket. On his back, his mother—whom he would never see again—had strapped a paper parcel with his belongings."

At once Dr. Clarke made arrangements to care for these children. Several years earlier, CCF had begun a cooperative effort with the famous SOS Homes. Scattered throughout Austria, they had helped to care for the youngsters whose fathers and mothers had been killed in World War II. One of these Homes was high up in the Tyrolean Alps, just outside the picturesque town of Imst, where the SOS Children's Village had been established. In every one of the twenty-odd houses that compose this "village" lives a family of ten children, each with its own "mother." Originally, there had been little folks from the Displaced Persons Camps of Fiestritz and Wagara, youngsters whose fathers had been killed in the war and whose mothers had died in the infamous Dachau. Others were orphans from the bombing of Vienna. A few were war babies—offspring of the occupying armies—deserted and unloved. At this and the other five CCF-affiliated Homes, Dr. Clarke cooperated with the superintendents in admitting the Hungarian waifs. Their occupancy soon doubled from this added strain, but new facilities were quickly added to accommodate them all.

This, then, was some of the European turmoil that prompted the burgeoning CCF growth. Meanwhile in southeastern Europe, 35 per cent of Greece's people were classified as destitute. Over a third of the people existed on an income less than $8 a month. During the war 13,500 villages were completely or partially destroyed. Livestock and capital goods were ruthlessly obliterated. In addition to wartime destruction there were natural disasters causing untold havoc. For example, on March 12, 1957, Dr. Clarke received a telegram reading, "LAST WEEK'S EARTHQUAKE WHICH HIT GREECE AFFECTED FORTY-FIVE VILLAGES WRECKING OR DAMAGING FOUR THOUSAND HOMES LEAVING TWENTY-FIVE THOUSAND HOMELESS."

Help was sent from Richmond so that the children's suffering would be lessened there.

In France, torn by war and poverty, CCF sponsors "adopted 700 children, orphaned or deserted, who had been received into sixteen orphanages.

In far-off Finland, the little nation that had fought a bullying Russia to a standstill, the needs were great. By 1954, CCF was aiding six orphanages there. Most of them were children from the Karelian Isthmus which Russia had demanded in 1939 and had forced her tiny neighbor to surrender. Four hundred thousand Finns moved out of the ceded territory rather than live under Communism. They left behind them their farms, livestock and homes. In the bloody Russo-Finnish War that lasted from October 14, 1939 to March 12, 1940, tens of thousands of Finnish mothers and fathers were killed. Orphans by the hundreds stumbled through the snow, many of them dying. Although the brave little country struggled to regain its economic prosperity, its needs have been great ever since.

By 1961, CCF was assisting eighteen homes in Finland and a total of almost 500 youngsters. Among the many CCF orphanages that have been visited by American tourists all over the world, Finnish homes often receive the highest praise. One letter written in the middle fifties read:

Dear Dr. Clarke:

Last week I visited my "adopted" boy—Jaako Ruisaho in Meltauksen Lastenkoti, Meltaus, Finland. You will be interested to know that I was once a social worker in a child-placing agency in the State of Washington. I have never been in an orphanage where I felt such warmth of affection for the children, coupled with a homelike atmosphere. The orphanage operates on a limited budget as you know. In spite of this, it is clean and bright and a happy place for children to live. They are treated as individuals, their personalities are respected.

Jaako is a bright, responsive child—thrilled to have a visit and some gifts from me. I have promised to continue to send money for his support. He starts school this fall and if he does well through the years, I hope to see that he secures a college education in the U.S.

Thank you for allowing me to help in this good work of yours.

By 1961, Christian Children's Fund had increased its aid to eighty orphanages in Europe with a total of 4,587 children. "Yet there are so many more who need our help," said Dr. Clarke.

In addition to its help to these European children, CCF had begun to send assistance through its "adoption" plan to several hundred children in Africa. There, too, the conflicting pressures of "imperialism," Communism and nationalism were bruising the lives of many youngsters.

Meanwhile, so many requests for help had come to Dr. Clarke from the United States and the Western Hemisphere that by 1952 CCF "charity began at home."

FIFTEEN

From Sea to Shining Sea

"WHY go overseas to help children?" wrote one sponsor to Dr. Clarke in the spring of 1951. "We have plenty of youngsters in need right here at home." With the dislocation of American industry in depressed areas as well as automation and other factors, unemployment reached an all-time high in some southern states. In several districts, jobs were disappearing at the rate of 10 per cent a year.

One CCF mountain worker informed Richmond headquarters, "Unemployment has reached the low of depression years. There is a resulting increase in broken homes and the number of children born out of wedlock."

Another superintendent told Dr. Clarke, "Just from general observation, this whole area through these eastern mountains shows absolutely no improvement over conditions as they were five years ago."

In the spring of 1952, Dr. Clarke journeyed through much of this area to see the problem first hand. As he visited town after town and orphanage after orphanage, he was appalled by the pitiful sights of children, semistarved, ragged and rejected, "right here in America—the 'land of opportunity.'"

Some parents, driven by desperation or psychosis, perpe-

167

trated frightful crimes on their helpless tots. Telling of three children who had just been admitted to one orphanage, Dr. Clarke's horror showed through his reports:

"All three children were not only frequently whipped. They received many beatings, as the black eyes of the older boys especially showed. The little girl was treated worst of all. Her own mother had tied her wrists together with wire, blindfolded her and dragged her into a small room that was heated with a coal stove. As her mother thrashed her, the little screaming girl, in trying to dodge the lash, fell several times against the stove. The doctor told me she will carry the scars for life."

This was an extreme case, but there were hundreds of American children in the same geographical setting who were as dirty and ragged and unloved. Many, too, were being left at Homes that were already crammed to capacity.

Visiting another orphanage in Tennessee, Dr. Clarke was told by the superintendent, "We have one little girl here who is three years old. She still can't walk because her back was injured from a beating she received when she was two." He paused, and then with deep solemnity he said, "Dr. Clarke, there are a thousand boys and girls right here in this country who should be taken out of evil environments like that. If I only had sufficient funds, I would remove them all from the ignorance, depravity and degeneracy to which they are daily exposed."

Moving with decisiveness, CCF added several Homes to its "family" upon Dr. Clarke's return to Richmond. Some of the earlier orphanages were in the Kentucky mountains. There in the mining districts, the folk had suffered a sort of backwash of poverty while the main stream of prosperity swept by. Children were not attending school for a variety of reasons. Some youngsters did not even have a pair of overalls that were not punctured with so many rips and holes as to make them unfit to be seen in public. Others did not attend because of the indifference or, indeed, the active opposition of parents. Many were suffering from tuberculosis, malnutrition, and in some instances, actual starvation.

In the midst of such poverty and hard-to-believe conditions, one of the CCF-affiliates was the Faith Children's Home. It was conducted by two staunch young missionaries. One of the wholesome aspects of this orphanage was its relaxed climate. Dr. Clarke in describing it said, "Rather than a Children's Home, their set-up was like a big family and the children came and went as such. Little could be said for the buildings and less for the furnishings. But the atmosphere of the Home was wonderful. The children came in from the nearby school while I was there. The first thing I heard them say as they flocked about her was "Hi, Mom!"

The Home, located in a town called Bear Track, has some natural assets that are wonderful for these children who have come from such sordid backgrounds. There are 107 acres, thirty of which are under cultivation by the older boys. They also have an assorted selection of cows, pigs, and chickens. "I arrived about 11:30," Dr. Clarke related, "and the first thing I heard were the words, 'Now you must stay to lunch.' I was glad I did. I found good home-cooking that was passed around the table 'family-style.' The glasses overflowed with rich milk from their own farm and the vegetables and meat were delicious. I tried to contrast this with meals I had been served in some of the shacks in the neighborhood—tiny portions of corn meal and sow belly. I can still remember the sparkling eyes of those youngsters around the orphanage table!"

The children all pitch in after school and "keep house." The girls do the housework while the boys work the farm. There is a workshop for mechanics and woodworking. But above all, there is the unifying spirit of Christ that warms the entire Home.

Although this is typical of many of the modest mountain Homes aided by CCF sponsors, there are some very imposing ones as well. Some of these, on the beaten paths of southern commerce, have many of the problems that arise in population-centers. Through the cities and town pass the "truckloads of children." They are white, Negro, Mexican, Puerto Rican, but they peer out wistfully at the lawns and schools of their luckier brothers and sisters. The wheezing trucks carry them to the current crop where they must pick vegetables or fruit for ten hours a day. There seem to be no Child Labor Laws to prevent it or if there are they are not enforced.

Some of them have families, many broken by divorce or desertion. Their only toys are beetles or sticks and stones. Every day these tots are exposed to drunkenness, violence and immorality. For lunch, they get a bottle of Coca-cola and a handful of crackers. They work in the hot sun from dawn to dusk with little respite, usually in a stooping position.

Some of these children have been deserted in southern towns like Greenville, Mobile, and Atlanta. Others have been subjected to such outrageous abuse that even somnolent courts have been stirred to action.

Into one of the CCF-affiliated homes in South Carolina recently came one girl of fourteen, a ward of the court. Her mother had been "renting" this child to as many as fourteen men in a night, Two others, a brother and sister who were victims of a broken home, had been found sleeping in a Greenville alley. Still another, Jerry, was dangerously upset because he had had twelve different "placements" in six years. His mother, a woman of easy virtue, returned periodically to claim him, keep him for a few months, and then deserted him again. Taken into a Greenville home he was at first extremely hostile, "rejected in the extreme." The love of the superintendent and the happy atmosphere of the other children has brought a new security into his life.

In 1961 the number of orphanages in the United States where over 1,000 children had been "adopted" by CCF sponsors had risen to 21. They were in ten states and ranged as far north as Pennsylvania, as far south as Florida and as far west as Arizona.

By that time, however, there were other Americans who were receiving CCF care. They were Americans who had suffered at the hand of the white man for over 400 years. Because of poor nutrition, exposure and neglect, the children of the American Indian were dying of measles, according to the Bureau of Indian Affairs, at a rate twenty times that of the non-Indian population. Nine times as many Indian youngsters were contracting tuberculosis as were white children. There were four times as many deaths from pneumonia and influenza. Three times as many Indian babies died at birth as their white brothers and sisters.

Into Arizona, Oklahoma, New Mexico, and South Dakota where the majority of reservation Indians live, Dr. Clarke sent CCF investigators in 1953 and 1954. They found distressing conditions both on and off the reservations.

"One family was typical of hundreds of others," reported one of these staff-members. "Among the Navajoes, I found a family living in a log 'hogan' so decrepit that I could see daylight through the walls. The children hauled water from a well a half-mile away. The father was earning $10 a week at odd jobs. Sometimes he and his family gather everything up and move with the migrants picking fruit. The father commented to me laconically, 'My kids don't have a chance!' "

To "give the kids a chance," Dr. Clarke recommended the founding of CCF projects through which the children could be "adopted." In addition, staff members brought Indian mission centers to his attention. One of these, the Holbrook

Navajo Mission School, was struggling to care for 135 children. Upon investigation, it was discovered that these youngsters were not only Navajo but also came from the Pima, Hopi, Apache, Sioux, Papago and Maricopa tribes. Although they sprang from different tribal origins, the distresses that brought them to the Holbrook Mission were tragically similar.

Case-histories that came to Richmond and were sent on to the "adopting" parents read: "The mother of this little kiddie is dead. The father is trying to support a large family but cannot find enough work. He cannot read or write. There is not enough food for all. The baby girl was brought to us."

"The father of this little Hopi boy is dead," read another. "The few sheep which were the family's source of income were stolen. The family was broken up and this youngster was brought to us."

Fragments from other case-reports told a similar tale: "Mother has TB. The children lack warm clothing" . . . "The land is poor—there will be little to store against a bitter winter" . . . "Mollie, age ten, is a 'sacrifice girl'—can't go to school—must stay at home and work" . . . "White step-father antagonistic to children—placed in the mission for protection" . . . "So weak couldn't walk when she came to us" . . . "Baby covered with sores and vermin."

Situated on a tract of 320 acres, the Mission School at Holbrook was founded by missionaries of the Seventh Day Adventist Church in 1946. Through added help from CCF and other sources, the Home was able to erect an excellent school building, dormitories and staff houses. Workshops, a power plant and other facilities were slowly added. The children received good training in many fields. The boys go forth as capable mechanics, carpenters, electricians. The girls prove to be excellent housekeepers, cooks, office workers. Some, because of their excellent background, go on to become trained nurses.

But all is not work at the Mission School. "Their happy

laughter is a tonic," wrote one CCF worker. "When I think of their original misfortune, rejection or bereavement, what contrast to their present fun on their swings and slides, their baseball diamonds and volley-ball courts!"

CCF sponsors of the 2,000 Indian children now under the "adoption" plan often visit the Homes and projects. "Rose-Mary is just one of the family," said Mrs. Peterson of Chicago in a letter to Dr. Clarke recently. "My heart swelled with happiness as I looked into her bright button eyes!" John Cooke, writing of his Pima lad, said, "I have never had more fun than when with Jack on the reservation last week."

Many sponsors of these red-skinned children, upon receiving their first letter from Dr. Clarke, feel as excited as if they have just experienced the birth of a new child. In the *Los Angeles Mirror* in 1960, appeared the story of a happy couple from that city. They had chosen to "adopt" a Papago Indian boy who lives on the reservation near Gila Bend in Arizona. Upon receiving the boy's picture and story, "I felt like passing out cigars," said the new "father." "It just seems as though he is away at school," said the "mother."

The CCF work among the American Indians has expanded so rapidly in the last few years that in late 1959, Dr. Clarke appointed a young missionary, Reverend C. W. Hardy, as regional director in the West. Because of the special needs, the work will undoubtedly grow even more in the near future.

"The poverty seems greater all the time," says Mr. Hardy. In a nation where the average per capita income is now over $2,000, the Navajo's average yearly earnings are less than $200. His food is only half of what he needs. His average weekly food bill is often only $2 and many have to subsist on less. If it were not for distribution of government surpluses they could not exist at all. As a result of this extreme poverty, the highest death rate in the United States is now found among the Navajoes.

As great as is the need here, however, the problems "south of the border" are even greater. Since 1954, "adoptions" among Latin American and West Indian children has increased fourfold. Now helping almost 1,000 youngsters in twenty-six orphanages in that part of the world, Dr. Clarke hopes for a Christian expansion of the Good Neighbor Policy. In *The Reader's Digest* in 1955 appeared a paragraph on Mexico: "When Vice-President Nixon visited Mexico he commented to President Ruiz Cortines about the beauty of the Presidential Mansion and the President of Mexico replied that, 'It is a beautiful mansion, Mr. Vice-President, but 300 metres away people live in caves.' That is the problem and tragedy of Mexico."

Dispatching Reverend Verent Mills to this area in early 1956, Dr. Clarke received a report that confirmed this problem. "The usual visitor," he wrote, "impressed with the new skyscraper hotels and other buildings in Mexico City, has no conception of how extremely poor and depressing is the existence of our Southern neighbors.

"Nowhere," he reported, "are all these unhappy circumstances more evident than on the streets of the city's Bowery. Dirty, ragged children swarm the pavements. They are barefoot, their clothing in shreds. Drunken wrecks, undisturbed by the swarms of flies crawling over them, are asleep in every direction you look. Tequilla or pulque, both very strong intoxicants made of the juice of cactus plants, are sold so cheaply that even beggars can buy all they want and they swill it in. Even many young children are already alcoholics.

"Several thousand homeless peasant boys live on the streets, begging, stealing from peddlers' carts, pawing through garbage cans. It gets cold at night in Mexico City, 7,500 feet high, and children sleep on the streets with perhaps an old newspaper or billboard 'ad' torn from a wall wrapped about them as their only covering.

"Many of Mexico's poorer children know only their first names. But rescued from the streets and given care in an orphanage, these Mexican children absorb a better way of life, like sponges!"

To prove this, Dr. Clarke authorized the opening of an orphanage at Guadalajara. There, with the help of Congregational missionaries, the Home started its operation in the Mesias Church. Furniture and equipment were gathered, property was secured, a small shed was added here, a room there, a playground leveled yonder. On the retirement of the missionary, Dr. Clarke appointed an American welfare worker named Miss Madge Smith. Under her direction it is a happy home!

"Every little bit of extra room helps," she told the Clarkes on a recent visit, "because the children keep coming to us—more and more—and it's almost impossible to turn them down!"

It is painful to "turn down" any children. Because of this, CCF sponsors now help to care for 374 additional youngsters in nine other Mexican homes that are run cooperatively with the Salvation Army.

The story of distress and need is the same farther south. In Boliva, Chile, and Brazil, as well as in the West Indian islands of Jamaica and in Puerto Rico, CCF has reached out arms of love to gather them in. There are special homes caring for blind youngsters. And there is an appealing home, run by a dedicated young lady named Sally Olsen, for the children of parents in prison. So anxious was she about these youngsters that when Dr. and Mrs. Clarke visited Puerto Rico in 1957, she was waiting on their hotel doorstep. From the desk of the International Hotel at the airport in San Juan came a phone call. "A lady from the prison wants to see you," said the clerk. "Send her up," replied Dr. Clarke impulsively. In a few minutes an attractive young woman entered. "I am Sally Olsen," she announced. "Then," said Dr. Clarke to me later, "I remembered. She was famous on the Island for her work among prisoners." Without preliminary she poured out the story of little boys and girls of San Juan.

" 'Why,' she asked finally, 'with all the work that is done for children, is there nothing being done for the children of prisoners? Just because a child's father is a thief, does that make his little boy or girl a thief?' " Stunned by her fervor, the Clarkes waited for more. "Sally's eyes became misty," recalled Mrs. Clarke, later. "I can't be complacent about them," Miss Olsen continued; "If you had visited these children, your heart would break. They are the sweetest kids. You would fall in love with them. I've dedicated my life to them. When I heard you were coming to Puerto Rico, I started praying that your CCF would help." Then Sally paused and took a deep breath. "Please, in His name, you must!"

Dr. and Mrs. Clarke did. Visiting the Rose of Sharon Home, their hearts were captured by the plain but orderly cottages, and the sparkle in the eyes of the boys and girls.

"Fortunately," Dr. Clarke commented, "there are missionaries like Sally Olsen all over the world who are excellent ambassadors for our country as well as for God."

"CCF cooperates with the missionaries of over thirty denominations," he added. "I feel that Christian Children's Fund has made a real contribution to the world-wide church by adding to it almost 100,000 members. Sometimes overseas I have visited church services where more CCF children have been in attendance than regular adult members. Brought up under the influence of the average CCF Home, many of the children later become pillars in their local churches. This, I believe, is the best form of evangelism, for the children are being nurtured in the faith during their most formative years. However, I must say that I have always been opposed to overzealous pressure being exerted upon our children. I believe that a child grows best when he grows naturally into faith in our Lord."

Calling to my attention certain statistics from the Missionary Research Library in New York, he pointed out that there are nearly 30,000 American missionaries now serving abroad. They are often the free world's "advance guard" and best spokesmen for truth and democracy. Many of them have readily seen the importance of a continuing work among children by giving valuable service on CCF committees overseas as well as helping in the Homes themselves.

To point up the contribution being made by CCF to this effort for freedom and truth, Dr. Clarke also showed me a report from the U.S. Government's agency, The International Cooperation Administration. It recently released figures showing that among a group of fifty-six religious and secular agencies granted licenses by the Administration, CCF ranks seventh in the amount sent overseas for welfare work. Its contribution is exceeded only by Church World Service, Care, Catholic Relief Services, American-Jewish Joint Distribution Committee, Lutheran World Relief and Hadassah.

SIXTEEN

All Those Feet Under
Our Table

"There are times," said Dr. Clarke, in January of 1961, "that I feel like the little old woman who lived in a shoe—I have so many children I don't know what to do!" With the fantastic growth of CCF, by 1960 over 36,000 youngsters were receiving food, clothing and other assistance from at least 100,000 friends.

Over the years since 1938, another phenomenon had also developed. Many people had come to look upon Dr. Clarke as a combination of kindly father, minister, administrator, promoter, confessor and advice-to-the-lovelorn expert. Across his desk daily pass scores of letters that indicate people's trust in and love for this remarkable man and his wife. Epistles range from the simple and folksy to the sublime. Some write regularly telling him of their weekly schedules. Others have heartache to share. Some express pet peeves. Still others just want to "talk things out."

One lady from Montana, writing regularly, said in her July communication:

> I thought I would get a letter to you before this but since I have been home from Helena, I have been so busy. First it was my housework, then my garden work, and laundry and some

calling on the sick. There were strawberries to pick and can. I froze some and made jelly of some . . . I got so I could hardly get up to go to the next strawberry plant. So we got someone to come and pick them and gave them the berries. My legs are giving me trouble and I could hardly bend my knees . . . I finally went to the doctor . . . He said I had the kind of arthritis that old folks get . . ."

Other correspondence was at different levels. From an unhappy man in Oregon came the note:

Dear Sir:

I believe it is a shame and a crime that children are made to wear clothes when it is not necessary for protection. They would be healthier and happier without, would look better, and the money could be used for much better purposes. Steps should be taken to counteract this infliction. Persons should have a right to be natural. I hope you will consider this in future planning . . ."

Others have gone through deep waters, yet are bravely cheerful. One lady in the South wrote:

I am an elderly preacher's widow, earning my way by keeping some apartments for college students. Have just rented one apartment to a nice refined couple from Malaya doing graduate work here. I tell all my wonderful tenants that we must all be nice to them and make them see that Americans are their friends. Friendship is so needed in the world today. Our prayers go up for peace and good will to come to all mankind. God bless you in your work.

I had my Christmas greetings from my little "adoptee" and have answered it. She is in Japan.

Many letters, too, bring word of tragedy and personal loss. Almost every day brings letters of loved ones who have carried on despite personal harm or distress. Some have suffered fire, children injured, or harmful accidents. Others have been accosted, attacked, robbed. One man penned the following from New York:

Friday morning of January 15, I had a new experience for me. I went to bed very late; I did not lock my room door. In the morning I found my billfold on the floor. I thought it was strange. I opened it and found that $60.00 which was in it when I went to bed was gone and no clue whatsoever. So I had only $1.50 left in my purse . . . I only write this to explain why I could not send the "adoption" payment for my little boy in Hong Kong before now . . .

These letters are a sampling of the many received and answered by Dr. and Mrs. Clarke in the stream of mail that flows through the Richmond office. In addition to handling the thousands of letters, of course, there is editing, ad-writing, and world-wide administration to keep the Clarkes busy. The two make a perfect team and a unique partnership.

Once Dr. Clarke related, "Mrs. Clarke sometimes tells me that I am an 'intrepid, reckless adventurer' sailing out in an uncharted sea with my boat overloaded to the gunwhales with children and babies but that somehow I find a harbor for them. She flatters, of course, and I am afraid I would be less daring if I did not know she would bail water, patch leaks that sprung, and see to it that none of our charges fell overboard!"

But Mrs. Clarke does far more than bail water and mend leaks. She possesses three qualities seldom found in any one person: a remarkable administrative ability, a gifted pen (for she is a talented writer), and a sympathy and kindness for underprivileged, unhappy children that is as deep as the sea.

On her shoulders falls the administration of the complex machinery that makes the international headquarters in Richmond run smoothly. There are the myriad problems of which few are aware. Each autumn her staff checks over 36,000 Christmas cards individually hand-made by the children and letters written by the children that are to be sent to the sponsors. There is the collating, instructing, advising, correcting and the guidance and direction of regional offices and homes around the world. It is she who avoids the slip-ups that might occur because of the mountain of work entailed in caring for 418 orphanages in forty-eight countries. Thus, Mrs. Smith gets the Christmas material prepared by her own child who lives in Africa below the equator and not from some other child who is in Lapland above the Arctic Circle.

Into her office come the many special requests of sponsors. "I would like to send my Japanese girl through college," writes one sponsor from St. Louis. "How much will this cost and how do I go about it?" Mrs. Clarke's staff goes to work immediately to coordinate this educational adventure for yet another young person—in 1961 hundreds of sponsors were providing college education for their "adopted" children.

"Please tell me," asks a lady from Buffalo, "how I can arrange for an eye operation for my little blind boy in Korea." At once, plans are set in motion for the engagement of an eye surgeon and the reservation of a hospital bed.

"Is there any way that I could see my child in the Philippines when I visit there next fall?" inquires one. A letter is sent forthwith to the superintendent of the Manila Children's Garden—"Please extend every courtesy to Mrs. Johnson when she visits . . ."

In addition to these two beloved leaders of CCF, there are the thousands of staff members working on five continents. Almost 3,000-strong, these faithful folk—house-mothers, superintendents, regional supervisors, executive secretaries, nurses, doctors, teachers—have won the hearts of vast numbers of children and the lasting friendship of grateful adults. A conservative estimate of the total number of youngsters who have been loved and cared for in CCF-owned or CCF-affiliated homes for the past twenty-three years is well in excess of 100,000. Each one of these tiny ambassadors has at one time or another been "adopted" by an American sponsor. Each of these children in his country has told and re-told the kindness of some far-away Yankee who helped to build the bridge of brotherhood by saving his life.

A close friend of CCF startlingly pin-pointed one American's personal contribution by saying to me, "Dr. Clarke has raised in the neighborhood of $100,000,000 in the cause of little children and others over the past fifty years!"

"Why," asked a letter to Dr. Clarke from a New Jersey man last July, "with such a record—a lifetime of faithful service for children—don't you and Mrs. Clarke retire? You deserve some rest and relaxation after all you have done to save little lives."

As Dr. Clarke read this letter to me, he said, "I would certainly like to retire. Nothing would please me better than to take down my fishing rod and live by the seashore. But," he shook his head thoughtfully, "I can't. Did you know that there are five hundred million youngsters who go to bed hungry every night? . . . Half the world's children—starving . . ." With such a challenge, could anyone say enough had been done, could anyone conscientiously say . . .

The End?